REJECTING
RELIGION

Embracing
Grace

BY GREG ALBRECHT

Published by Plain Truth Ministries, Pasadena, CA

Unless otherwise indicated, all Scripture passages are
from the Holy Bible, New International Version (NIV)
copyright ©1973, 1978, 1984 by International Bible Society.
Used by permission of Zondervan Publishing House.
All rights reserved.

Library of Congress Cataloging-in-Publication Data

Albrecht, Greg. 1947 -
Rejecting Religion: Embracing Grace /
Greg Albrecht

p. cm.
Includes biographical references and index.

Cover photo by rgbspace/iStockphoto

ISBN-978-1-889973-10-4

1. Theology, Doctrinal—Popular works.
2. Christianity—Miscellanea
I. Title

Contents

INTRODUCTION   4
ACKNOWLEDGEMENTS   8

Chapter One
WHO IS GOD AND WHO IS OUR NEIGHBOR?   10

Chapter Two
IT'S SHOW TIME! (*Matthew 23:5-12*)   18

Chapter Three
THE KINGDOM—THE CURE... (*Matthew 23:13*)   31

Chapter Four
THE HELL OF IT ALL (*Matthew 23:15*)   52

Chapter Five
BLIND LEADING THE BLIND (*Matthew 23:16-22*)   74

Chapter Six
WAITER—THERE'S A CAMEL IN MY SOUP!
(*Matthew 23:23-24*)   90

Chapter Seven
MIGHT AS WELL PUT LIPSTICK ON A PIG
(*Matthew 23:25-28*)   111

Chapter Eight
RELIGION GONE WILD (*Matthew 23:29-36*)   127

Chapter Nine
A NEVER-ENDING RIVER OF LIVING WATER
(*Matthew 23:37-39*)   143

Chapter Ten
EMBRACING GRACE   159

*M*y computer screen flickered for a moment, and then the video my friend from Indiana sent me started to play. An ordinary guy was sitting in front of his computer screen—he looked at me and said: "I got an email the other day which said...*Jesus loves you.*"

Ordinary guy thought "that's nice," but then he read the rest of the email, which said... "*If you don't start doing what Jesus says you're going to burn in hell forever.*"

Ordinary guy pondered... "So, this love Jesus has for me is conditional. I can understand that. Love has conditions attached. That's the way I understand love. When we got married I loved my wife [picture of gorgeous young woman posing by a swimming pool]. But then she gained some weight [picture of the same woman, older, having gained a lot of weight, eating snacks while watching television] so I stopped loving her. Now we're divorced. I know. I'm shallow. But somehow I thought Jesus would be different.

Ordinary guy wrote back to this Christian..."If Jesus loves me, why does he want to send me to hell?"

He got this reply... "*He doesn't want to, but if you don't accept him he has to.*"

Bewildered, ordinary guy took his eyes off his computer screen and stared into space, wrestling with his dilemma: "I'm confused. Doesn't Jesus make the rules? Surely if he doesn't want to do something he doesn't have to."

The world of Christendom at large misrepresents Jesus, because it has been overcome by religion. Ordinary guy doesn't realize it, but the problem is not Jesus—it's religion! The problem is that many believe religion is the answer, when religion is actually the problem.

Why is religion the problem?
• Religion defines God as upset and angry, looking for ways to punish us—a God whom we must appease and please by our efforts. Yes, God loves us, says religion, but the divine love it proclaims is conditional.
• Religion is the almost universally accepted notion that human performance gains a higher standing with God.
• Religion consists of programs and practices that promise the reward of heaven in return for our good deeds and the punishment of hell in return for our failures.

- Religion is dispensed by professionals who prescribe potions and programs which they say will fix and cure us.
- Religion insists that the degree to which God will love us is up to us.

It is true that religion can also be defined as an ordered, systematic way of understanding and following God. According to the Bible there is such a thing as pure religion (James 1:27) but that passage also means that there is such a thing as impure religion. Sadly, much of what passes for religion within modern Christendom is far from the pure, unadulterated grace of God.

The religion that thrives within Christendom reduces Jesus to a behavior-modification program, sin-management that replaces God's grace with human performance. Christless religion is something that one does, for the purpose of keeping God's punishment at bay. Legalistic religion begins with the premise that God's blessings are achieved through a diligent program of performing prescribed practices.

Oppressive religion makes a spiritual diagnosis, offers medications and remedies, with the promise of spiritual healing and recovery provided its regimen is carefully (religiously) maintained and observed. When God's grace is ripped out of Christianity, grace-less religion is left, with all of its protocols and prescriptions.

As I write, the Gulf of Mexico is awash in a huge oil slick, the Deepwater Horizon disaster, reported to be the largest offshore spill in U.S. history. This catastrophe started when an unexpected methane gas bubble burst from the well and exploded on a drilling rig. Grace-less religion is similar—volatile, toxic gas billows out of religious institutions in the form of mandates, dogma and fundamentalist *fatwas*, wreaking havoc and destruction.

Like oil spills, religion leaves an ugly residue in its wake—sticky, tarry gunk that you can't seem to get rid of. Christ-less religion contaminates the very souls of those who expect it to cleanse and heal. Those who have long-term relationships with religion find it nearly impossible to escape its grimy clutches.

If you've heard that Jesus loves you, but he's going to condemn you to hell if you don't accept him (because he has to)—I have good news for you. *In the chapters that follow we will contrast the purity of God's grace with the corruption of institutionalized, Christ-less religion.* We'll examine what Jesus has to say about religion, especially in Matthew 23.

We'll discover that Jesus reserved his most caustic invective for religious practices and teachings which beguile and enslave. He is the Lord our Shepherd, and in that role he denounces the addictive pills, potions, programs and procedures prescribed by religious professionals.

Jesus was rejected by established religion because he refused to align himself with it. In our first chapter we'll study the parable of the Good Samaritan, and how Jesus cast himself in a role that was and is despised and rejected by religion.

We'll carefully study what Jesus has to say about the kingdom of religion, and by comparison, what he has to say about the kingdom of heaven. Signature passages from Matthew 23 will introduce many of our chapters, and we'll see that Jesus uses words like *woe, hypocrites, blind, greed, self-indulgent, unclean, desolate, hell* and *snakes* to describe the religious industry, its professionals and the consequences it brings into the lives of those it "serves."

Of course, Jesus doesn't just bash religion without offering an answer. We will see that Jesus invites us to a live bold, passionate life of freedom—a new and transformed life he lives within us. By God's grace, we can be cleansed from the religious globs of tar that stick to our souls like oil spills pollute the physical environment.

The cleansing agent whereby our hearts and souls can be purified of all filth, whether physical or religious, is called grace. What is grace? It's compassion. Gratitude. Generosity. Faith. Humility. Surrender. Service.

Grace cannot be acquired on the basis of a *quid-pro-quo* transaction—grace can only be received, as a gift. Grace cannot be purchased. Grace cannot be found through endless study and knowledge of the Bible. Grace can't be cloned. Religion can't replicate grace, though it does its best to provide clever counterfeits.

Living by God's grace, compared to institutionalized religion, is like coloring outside the lines. Christendom has done its best to package relationship with God in spiritual paint-by-the-numbers exercises, but God's grace provides freedom in Christ—freedom from religion.

God's grace and his love are intertwined—joined at the hip. You can't have one without the other. God *is* love. He doesn't just *have* love—love is what God *is*.

God's grace delivers and expresses his love. God's grace, like his love, has no limits or boundaries. Grace defies logic and even offends our sense of fair play. The implications of grace are staggering—scandalous—outrageous.

Christ-less religion has erected its institutions, cathedrals, mosques, synagogues, temples and churches. Christ-less religion has its treasured icons of rituals, customs and ceremonies. But out of the ocean of God's love, wave after wave of his grace relentlessly erodes the un-grace of religion. The never-ending waves of God's grace will eventually cover the shifting sands of the kingdom of religion as the waters cover the sea.

Dietrich Bonhoeffer, a 20th century Christian martyr who was killed by the Nazis because of his faith in Christ, said that "Jesus calls men, not to a new religion, but to life!"

Billions of people in our world today are spiritually dead thanks to poisonous, lethal religion. The good news is that Jesus did not start another religion. Jesus did not come to make bad people better. He came to make spiritually dead people live!

*T*he idea for this book first gained traction during one of the many free-form brainstorming sessions I enjoy with my good friend and co-worker, Monte Wolverton. Monte is a gifted artist, an accomplished musician and a cartoonist. He oozes creativity. As my right-hand man for many years, Monte has challenged my thinking and offered fresh perspectives.

After initial discussions with Monte, the original ideas started to take root, and the fermentation process started. I will not attempt, for various reasons, to mention all those who contributed to the ongoing creative process. A collective "thank you" to those whose ideas and insights influenced and inspired me through the many drafts of the manuscript.

As phrases, paragraphs and pages evolved, my wife Karen started her early edits and suggestions, as she read many of the early drafts. Karen is my partner, for this book, my ministry in general and in the life and love we have shared for over 41 years.

Laura Urista wears many hats at PTM, fulfilling important roles in our ongoing work. Laura joined in proofreading, input my handwritten edits in early stages and assisted me with all of the necessary details, helping to transform the manuscript into the book you now hold in your hands.

Marv Wegner and Phyllis Duke were also part of our team. Phyllis, as she has for many of my other books, supplied typing and proofreading skills. Marv contributed layout and graphic features—not the least of which was our cover. Thanks to each of you for your critically important contributions—Monte, Karen, Laura, Phyllis and Marv.

It is customary that one or at most two names adorn the cover and spine of a book. My name is on the book, and I will take the primary responsibility for what is said herein.

All that said, I thank God for his amazing grace, enabling me to offer some insights and shed some light on the kingdom of heaven. Thank God that the kingdom of religion will one day come to an end, and thank God that his kingdom of heaven will endure forever!

*F*or Karen: During the final stages of this book you endured your second surgery for cancer, followed by a long, painful series of radiation treatments. It's been a tough year, which God has enabled you to face courageously and bravely.

While we have lived 34 of our 41 years of marriage in the same house, our real home wasn't constructed with nails or bricks. Our true home doesn't have doors or windows, because it's with each other—and our eternal home is, by God's grace, in the kingdom of heaven.

You will forever be my *Unchained Melody.*

Who Is God and Who Is Our Neighbor?

*A*s parents and grandparents we smile at stories about children getting confused about God:

During Jason's bedtime prayer he said, "Lord, if you can't make me a better boy, don't worry about it. I'm having a real good time like I am."

Sarah complained to God that he did not answer her prayer. "Thank you for the baby brother but what I asked for was a puppy. I never asked for anything else before. You can look it up."

Lisa pondered the nature of God when she prayed, "How do you know you are God? Did someone tell you, or did you just decide that yourself?"

Bobby was sitting in the back seat of the car as he and his parents were on their way home from church. Bobby was really quiet, so his parents starting asking him about Sunday school. Bobby finally said that he was worried about what the Sunday school teacher had said. "She said that she hoped we would all grow up in Christian homes. But I want to stay with you guys."

We adults are tempted to assume that since we are all "grown up" that we completely understand God, and for that matter, each other. But that's not really the case, is it? The older we get the more we understand how much we have misunderstood both God and our neighbors here on planet earth. Getting older is no guarantee that we will automatically come to know all there is to know about God or our neighbors.

When we lived in England my wife and I had some "funny ha-ha" and "funny embarrassing" experiences getting to know a different culture. You may have heard that England and the United States are two countries separated by a common language. Because the British speak the same (or at least nearly the same) language, we often feel like we're next-door neighbors. But my wife and I learned quickly that the same words can have entirely different meanings to a "Yank" or a "Brit," and that idioms in either the Queen's English or American English are not always understood in the same way. These misunderstandings can cause even next-door neighbors to misunderstand each other.

Many years ago one of our English friends was planning to stop by our apartment one evening, so earlier in the day he said, "Would it be all right if I knock you up about seven this evening?" He obviously didn't know that "knocking up" someone in American English involved far more than merely knocking on their front door. I smiled and explained why I would not welcome him "knocking me up" at any time!

There are hilarious examples about American companies attempting to market their products to other cultures. When General Motors first introduced the Chevrolet Nova in South America, it had no idea that "no va" in Spanish means "it won't go." The model was renamed. Ford had a car which didn't do so well in Latin America either—it was named the Fiera, which translates into "ugly old woman." Kentucky Fried Chicken discovered that their slogan "finger-lickin' good" comes out as "eat your fingers off" in Chinese.

Of the many mistranslations I have heard, one of my

favorites was a sign posted in a hotel in India. Tourists were concerned about the tap water, so management assured them, "All water has been personally passed by the management."

There are many examples of misunderstandings within the world of religion—both of God and of our neighbors.

According to Matthew and Luke, the greatest commandment in the law is to love the Lord with all your heart and with all your soul and with all your strength and with all your mind, and to love your neighbor as yourself (Matthew 22:37-39; Luke 10:27; see also Deuteronomy 6:5; Leviticus 19:18). Is obedience to this greatest commandment required of us so that God will love us in return? Within Christendom, there is a great deal of misunderstanding about God's love. How can we love God and our neighbor, and beyond that, how can we know the one true God and how can we know who exactly is our neighbor? The parable of the Good Samarian answers these questions, as it illustrates how Jesus fulfilled the law (Matthew 5:17):

Luke 10:29-30: "But he wanted to justify himself, so he asked Jesus, 'And who is my neighbor?' In reply Jesus said: 'A man was going down from Jerusalem to Jericho, when he fell into the hands of robbers. They stripped him of his clothes, beat him and went away, leaving him half dead.'"

Jesus told the story of The Good Samaritan, one of his most beloved and well-known parables, as an answer to a question posed to him by a man Luke identifies as "an expert in the law" (Luke 10:25). The first question the expert in the law asked Jesus concerned what must be done to inherit eternal life (Luke 10:25). Notice the emphasis—what *must I do*? What deeds *must I fulfill*? What rituals *must be performed*? What laws *must be obeyed*? What ceremonies *must I observe?*

Jesus threw the question back to this expert in the law, and asked him what the law said. The man quoted the great law, which says to love God and love your neighbor. Luke comments that this religious leader wanted "to justify himself" (Luke 10:29)—he assumed he could demonstrate his love for God by keeping the law. He wanted to make sure he knew the precise identity of his neighbor, so that he could make sure that he loved the right person, thus fulfilling his obedience to the law. As religious legalists always do, *the expert in the law wanted the exact legal requirements he needed to fulfill.* So the "expert in the law" asked his second question—"Who is my neighbor?"

In response, Jesus told him a story about a man traveling on a dangerous road from Jerusalem to Jericho who was robbed, beaten, stripped of his clothing and left for dead. Jesus shocked the expert in the law and the others who heard this story with the roles he assigned to the good guy who helped the wounded man and the bad guys who would not. The good guy in the parable was a Samaritan, and the two bad guys were respected Jewish religious leaders.

To use the word "good" and "Samaritan" in the same breath was as religiously scandalous to that original audience as it would be today for Muslims to hear a sermon titled "The Good Jew" in a conservative mosque. Of all people, the Samaritan was the most unlikely person—the person least likely to be thought of in that society as a kind and considerate person—yet it was the Samaritan who stopped to help the man who had been left for dead. It's hard for us to imagine how much the Jews of that day hated and detested the Samaritans.

The Jews saw the Samaritans as a mixed-blood race—their heritage going back to intermarriages between the exiles from the northern kingdom and the gentiles imported into the land by the Assyrians (2 Kings 17:24). The Jewish religion perceived Jews as racially pure, the only true, chosen people of God, unlike their second-class Samaritan relatives, who were considered to be spiritual half-breeds. Furthermore the Samaritans had constructed their own temple on Mount Gerizim (as contrasted with the Jewish temple in Jerusalem). Centuries of hatred, prejudice and bigotry formed the background of the Jewish-Samaritan ill will in the time of Jesus.

While the hero of Jesus' parable was a despised Samaritan, Jesus assigned the role of the bad guys to the highly respected religious leaders (the same profession as the expert in the law who asked the question prompting Jesus to give this parable!) In Jesus' story the revered religious leaders saw the wounded man, and "passed by on the other side" of the road. The man suffering on the side of the road was stripped of his clothes and appeared to be "half dead" (Luke 10:30). He could not be identified as someone who "deserved" to be helped on the basis of his clothing—he was naked. He couldn't be identified by his language, accent or dialect—he was "half dead" and unable to speak.

Here was someone who could not be identified as a member of "our nationality," "our side" or "our church." The man who had been left half dead was *just a human being.* Imagine that. This person, regardless of appearances and affiliations, which could not be immediately discerned, was just as loved by God as any other human being.

We often, in reading this parable, think of Jesus as the Good Samaritan, as well we should. But then we go on and think that Jesus is giving us this parable so we will know the efforts in which we should engage so that we can earn Jesus' love. We've heard sermons telling us about how Jesus wants us to help the less fortunate. We're told to follow the Good Samaritan's example. *We assume that the real lesson Jesus is teaching us in this parable is that we should determine to help those in need, even those really-hard-to-like people who don't talk or look like us.*

But we forget that the parable of the Good Samaritan doesn't stand alone. In order to understand what Jesus was teaching, we must understand the context. Jesus gave the parable in response to two questions by the expert in the law: **1)** "what must I do to inherit eternal life?" (Luke 10:25) and **2)** "...who is my neighbor?" (Luke 10:29).

Thinking that the parable of the Good Samaritan tells us *what we need to do* takes us into the same spiritual pitfall which trapped the expert in the law. The parable of the Good Samaritan is not about the efforts we must exert to be good Samaritans, it's about Jesus—*the* Good Samaritan!

When we think of the Good Samaritan from a Christ-centered, grace-based perspective, we can see that Jesus was saying that he was and is the only one who can do for us what we cannot do for ourselves. Jesus will do for us what many busy religious professionals will not even attempt to do for us.

We are the battered, bruised man for whom the religious leaders would not stop. Jesus, discredited in the eyes of religion just as much as a Samaritan was rejected in the eyes of the Jews of the first century, is our unlikely healer. Jesus did not give himself the respectable role of priest or pastor here. This is not the parable of the Good Priest or the Good Pastor or the Good Minister. In fact, this parable did not carry the title "Good" Samaritan when Jesus first gave it. For that first century religious audience, there was no such thing as a good Samaritan.

The parable of the Good Samaritan answers the question posed by the expert in the law, "who is my neighbor?" *The answer Jesus gives to that question is not primarily intended to give you directions about what you need to do to be a good neighbor.* The lesson of the Good Samaritan is about what Jesus has done, is doing and will always do. He is the only one who truly cares. He is the only one who can truly heal and make you whole. He will do for you what religion cannot and will not do.

Eternal life does not come from religious professionals—many of them will pass by on the other side of the road (Luke 10:31). Spiritual healing and eternal life comes from the despised carpenter from Nazareth. The real Jesus, who brings the fullness of grace (John 1:16), is still despised and rejected by religion now (Isaiah 53:3) just as it then discredited the Good Samaritan.

Jesus answered the first question asked by the expert in the law—"what must I do to inherit eternal life?" (Luke 10:25) by calling his attention to the two great commandments, love God and love your neighbor. Jesus answered the second question asked by the expert in the law "...who is my neighbor?" (Luke 10:29) with the parable.

According to the parable, religious leaders (like the expert in the law) neglected people like the man who was robbed and beaten and left half dead. Jesus depicted pious religious authorities as reluctant to "waste their time" serving those in need. But, as hard as it was for religious leaders to help such an unfortunate individual, which neighbor would have been more difficult for them to love: **1)** the man who was robbed, beaten and left half dead, or **2)** the Samaritan who stopped to help the man the religious leaders passed by?

It is easier to fulfill a list of requirements and in so doing feel you have "loved your neighbor" than it is to love Jesus, the Good Neighbor! Loving Jesus means loving God's grace, the very thing that religion despises, just as it then detested the Samaritan.

Simply stated, the lesson of the Good Samaritan is to love our neighbor, (Jesus) and to love God (Jesus—God with us, God in the flesh). God is both our God and our neighbor, and in loving him we fulfill, as Jesus did and does, the law. Jesus is the fulfillment of the law! (Matthew 5:7).

This is not to say that Christ-followers will ignore the needs of the less fortunate. Because we are in Christ and he is in us, we will stop and help those who are in need. If we truly love Jesus, if we truly surrender to him, then because we love our divine Neighbor (Jesus, God in the flesh), we will love our physical neighbors who are in need. Jesus instructed those who follow him to meet the needs of those who are hungry, thirsty, sick, homeless, imprisoned and without adequate clothing (Matthew 25:34-36). Jesus was not only talking about those who have physical needs, he was talking about those who are spiritually hungry and thirsty—those who are spiritually homeless and in spiritual bondage.

Jesus said *"whatever you did for one of the least of these brothers of mine, you did for me"* (Matthew 25:40). Whether we help or don't help those in need is not the criteria of eternal life. Because Christ lives his risen life in and through us we will certainly help others. But the real issue is in whose name and by what power we do so.

The kingdom of God is given by grace, for love. The kingdom of heaven is about Jesus. It is his presence, his peace and his rest. We are given the kingdom by grace. We don't earn the kingdom by helping the needy. However, once we are given the kingdom, there is no question that we will help the needy, for the kingdom of heaven transports us into God's spiritual dimension. We serve others because that's what Jesus did, does and forever will do.

The parable of the Good Samaritan has Jesus in the role of the despised Samaritan, the person who, in the minds of the good, synagogue-going, commandment-keeping audience who first heard the parable, was highly unlikely as well as unqualified to render aid of any kind. The two characters Jesus cast as the most obvious and qualified to help were a priest and a Levite—highly respected religious leadership roles within Judaism.

At the end of the parable of the Good Samaritan Jesus asked the expert in the law, "Which of these three do you think was a neighbor to the man who fell into the hands of robbers?"

The answer was and is obvious. The expert in the law could not bring himself to even say the word "Samaritan"—so he simply said, "The one who had mercy on him" (Luke 10:37). Who was and is the true neighbor? Jesus is the one and only Good Samaritan.

In this story Jesus reveals that if we truly love him he will enable us to love the neighbor we would otherwise love the least. He became that neighbor—he is *the* good Samaritan. We love God and our neighbor by focusing our heart, mind and soul on Jesus, who is God in the flesh. Forget the religion, focus on Jesus.

Chapter 2

It's Show Time!

"Everything they do is done for men to see: They make their phylacteries wide and the tassels on their garments long; they love the place of honor at banquets and the most important seats in the synagogues; they love to be greeted in the marketplaces and to have men call them 'Rabbi.' But you are not to be called 'Rabbi,' for you have only one Master and you are all brothers. And do not call anyone on earth 'father,' for you have one Father, and he is in heaven. Nor are you to be called 'teacher,' for you have one Teacher, the Christ. The greatest among you will be your servant. For whoever exalts himself will be humbled, and whoever humbles himself will be exalted."—Matthew 23:5-12

During World War II the American and British military brought the material goods of their culture into the remote islands of the South Seas. These civilizations had never experienced the wealth and prosperity enjoyed by the powers that had recently arrived to occupy their land. When the war was over, the military bases were closed, and there were no more shipments of the material resources to which the inhabitants of these islands had become accustomed.

The lifestyle of the islanders drastically changed. Up until the end of the war some of the soldiers shared medicine, canned food, radios, tents and clothing with the islanders. The locals had become accustomed to crates descending out of the sky, filled with Coca-Cola, candy, canned meat and all manner of riches and delicacies they had never known. Suddenly the supply of this heretofore-unheard-of treasure trove of resources dried up.

The islanders longed for the cargo which had once arrived by plane or by ship to reappear. In an effort to cause the resources to return, followers of what came to be called *cargo cults* started to mimic the activities they had observed the soldiers perform, thinking if they acted like the soldiers, the resources would return.

The islanders built landing strips where airplanes could land with the cargo they so longed for—hence the term cargo cults. They created replicas of headsets, carving wooden headphones adorned with bamboo antennas. The hand-crafted headsets were worn by cargo cult followers who sat in towers, seemingly functioning as air traffic controllers—for non-existent airplanes. They lit up the runways with signal fires and torches, hoping to attract night landings.

Hoping to cause the return of the cargo and merchandise they had once enjoyed, they staged drills and marches, with sticks substituting for rifles and military uniforms and insignias painted on the bodies of the cargo cult "soldiers." They believed that the occupying armies had some special and unique connection with the gods, and that something they did influenced the gods to rain down material blessings. The cargo cult followers seemed to be doing all of the right things. They had created, to the best of their abilities, the same form and appearance they had seen before—but of course to no avail, for the cargo did not materialize. No planes landed. No merchandise arrived.

In 2 Timothy 3:5 Paul warns of those who do not love the one true God, who have a form of godliness but deny its power. Religion can deceive us into thinking that the physical, outward, external form (what is seen and touched and felt) is more important than the spiritual, inner, unseen substance. The image that the eye sees is powerful, leading religion to motivate its followers by appearances. Jesus said that "everything" the teachers of the law and the Pharisees did was "done for men to see."

There are all kinds of "forms" of godliness that are alive and well within Christ-less religion today:

1) Ritual. Many feel that if they can just perform the right rituals and ceremonies and duties, in the right way at the right time, then God will bless them with health and wealth—and conversely he won't curse them. Shades of the cargo cult!

2) Attendance. Many feel that if they just show up, assemble and attend—then that will make God happy. If they just march around in a "Christian" assembly, with their little stick rifles, in "God's Army" then that will keep God happy—at least for one more week when they will need to do it all over again.

3) Heritage. Many believe that they have a form of godliness because they were born into a particular religion or denomination. They believe that their religious club has "the truth" or "more truth" than anybody else. They belong to or frequent a particular spiritual address because it's the only thing they have ever known.

4) Liturgy. Many think candles, bells, stained glass windows, choirs, pipe organs, incense and chanting is what God wants, and if they engage in such "holy" behavior and worship then God is pleased. Others, who favor a more contemporary experience, feel if they raise their hands to lively music in an exercise called "praise and worship" then their "worship" will ensure that they know God.

The Bible speaks of empty, meaningless religion as being like wells without water. A religious well without water holds the promise of being able to quench thirst—but when the truth is finally realized, such an empty well is but a mockery. Christ-less religion is incapable of dispensing God's grace.

Apart from God, religious rituals and ceremonies are *secondhand spirituality*—humans merely going through the motions. Jesus makes it clear—if we are to have an authentic, real, vibrant relationship with God we must personally respond to him and allow him to transform us. Jesus uses the metaphor of being born spiritually, from above (John 3:3).

All forms of cargo cult religion are but a mockery. God is not influenced, conjured up or manipulated through machinations, obedience, rituals, uniforms, behaviors or practices. The power of God is not isolated to musical expression or devout prayer or outward appearance.

Believe it or not, every year in the Republic of Vanuatu a celebration is held, even to this day, with islanders clothed in what look like old United States Army fatigues and uniforms, marching with bamboo rifles slung across their shoulders. It's so obvious to sophisticated North Americans, isn't it? Cargo cult religion is primitive idolatry. Cargo cult religion is superstitious, oppressive religion that holds its people in spiritual captivity.

Religious Uniforms: Phylacteries and Tassels

The signature passage for this chapter serves as a prelude to the "seven woes" of Matthew 23. Before we consider the seven woes let's pause and consider the warning Jesus gave in the initial verses of Matthew 23. He cautions about the priority religion gives to concentrating on appearances, and in so doing, missing the real power of God that is often not visible to the naked eye.

Jesus warns about a pseudo-spiritual image that can be created by uniforms worn by religious professionals. Such attire creates a holier-than-thou atmosphere. Costumes can then become an essential part of the show, when religious business is conducted.

Most religions have distinctive "garb" or accessories which they use to distinguish and decorate its officials and leaders. Robes, vestments, habits and clerical collars are among those more familiar to most of us. The teachers of the law, Pharisees, Sadducees and priests of Jesus' day were no different. Jesus mentions two pieces of apparel used as clerical dress by Jewish religious leaders of his day. While religious trappings themselves have no "magical" powers, many attribute spiritual strength and supremacy to those who wear them.

Pictures of modern and ancient *phylacteries* can be found, online, via a request through a search engine. Orthodox Jewish men today still wear *phylacteries* or *tefillin*, small leather boxes containing selected texts from Exodus and Deuteronomy. Phylacteries are required by Jewish oral tradition to be worn during prayer. Two boxes are bound with leather straps, one to the forehead and one to the hand. Here is one of the texts typically contained in the boxes, the famous *Shema*—a Hebrew word that means *hear*:

Deuteronomy 6:4-8: *"Hear, O Israel: The LORD our God, the LORD is one. Love the LORD your God with all your heart and with all your soul and with all your strength. These commandments that I give you today are to be upon your hearts. Impress them on your children. Talk about them when you sit at home and when you walk along the road, when you lie down and when you get up. Tie them as symbols on your hands and bind them on your foreheads"* *(See also Exodus 13:9, 16; Deuteronomy 11:18).*

The Jewish oral traditions, later recorded in the *Mishna*, take this Deuteronomy 6:8 quote quite literally, and thus verses are bound to foreheads and hands with leather straps. You might not see examples of this practice in your day-to-day life. But in the world of orthodox Judaism, it is a daily occurrence.

You can see phylacteries being worn in many orthodox Jewish metropolitan areas in North America or Europe. Phylacteries are commonplace in synagogues, in places where orthodox Jews congregate throughout Israel, such as the Western Wall in Jerusalem, and on many El Al Airlines flights.

Jesus said that the teachers of the law and Pharisees made "their phylacteries wide and the tassels on their garments long." Bigger boxes and longer tassels were more than fashion statements in the religious hierarchy of Jesus' day. Jesus exposed the silliness of spiritual one-upmanship holiness contests, revealing them to be a façade of faith. Attributing special powers and status to those who bedeck themselves with spiritual uniforms is a sign of an outward religion, not an internal relationship.

Apparently the religious leaders of Jesus' day were purchasing and wearing bigger and fancier phylacteries to distinguish themselves in the practice of prayer. Do better boxes make prayers more effective? Does God pay keener attention to the prayers of those who wear broader phylacteries? It is laughable. But it was happening. According to Jesus, prayer competition among clergy is futile religious ambition. Religious arrogance and pride appalled Jesus.

Can bigger boxes change the human heart? Do bigger phylacteries make a religious leader a bigger and better man of God? Some apparently thought so. Jesus could not abide this spiritual obsession without scathing criticism.

It was the same thing with longer tassels. Orthodox Jewish men today still wear prayer shawls called a *tallit*. The tassels on each of its four corners are called *tzitzit*:

Deuteronomy 22:12: *"Make tassels on the four corners of the cloak you wear."*

You may remember the New Testament story of a woman with a hemorrhage being healed by touching the "edge" of Jesus' garment (Matthew 9:20-22; Mark 5:25-34; Luke 8:43-48). This was undoubtedly the *tzitzit*. It represents not only the ritual purity of the wearer, but also his authority as head of a family. Only family members were allowed to touch it. But Jesus calls the woman "daughter," thus, rather than condemning her for the act, he generously includes her in his spiritual family, as one coming under his household protection.

Thus, in a futile attempt to enhance their relationship with God, the Pharisees super-sized their phylacteries and the tassels on their prayer shawls.

Places of Honor and Important Seats

Jesus accused the Pharisees of loving "the most important seats in the synagogues." Once again, Jesus expresses his opposition to the love of appearances which religious author-ities can find attractive. The Pharisees loved being big cheeses. They loved being seen. They loved the spotlight. They loved the acclaim of men.

Within the religious culture of Jesus' day, seating at din-ners and banquets was assigned according to social rank. The host was seated in a place of honor, as were the most hon-ored guests. The closer you sat to the host, the higher your place in the social pecking order. Jesus accused the teachers of the law of coveting the best seats. As so often is the case in his ministry and teaching, Jesus indicates his preference for the precise opposite of prevailing practice and custom:

Luke 14:8-11: "When someone invites you to a wedding feast, do not take the place of honor, for a person more distinguished than you may have been invited. If so, the host who invited both of you will come and say to you, 'Give this man your seat.' Then, humiliated, you will have to take the least important place. But when you are invit-ed, take the lowest place, so that when your host comes, he will say to you, 'Friend, move up to a better place.' Then you will be honored in the presence of all your fellow guests. For everyone who exalts himself will be humbled, and he who humbles himself will be exalted."

Jesus is addressing pride in the human heart. Humble yourselves, he is saying. Forget the social symbols that play to your vanity and ego:

Matthew 23:12: "For whoever exalts himself will be humbled, and whoever humbles himself will be exalted."
Mark 9:35: "Sitting down, Jesus called the Twelve and said, 'If any-one wants to be first, he must be the very last, and the servant of all.'"

Jesus had a great deal to say about the futility of thrusting yourself into a place of prominence. It was one of the primary themes of his message. You cannot fake humility. You cannot act humble for the purpose of self-exaltation. Rather, Jesus is talking about a state of being. He is talking about the habits of a humble heart, imparted as a gift of God's grace.

So how do you kill the social ambition that poisons your heart? How do your overcome the normal human desire to be seen in places of prestige and to be esteemed by your peers as being important? If Jesus lives in you and you live in him he will help you to see the futility of trying to climb the ladder of human importance and prestige. Jesus, as he lives within you, will help you confront the ugliness of your own desperate arrogance.

After all, building your sense of self-worth on societal or religious position is a house built on sand. How much recognition is enough to prove your worth before God? How many accolades will quench your self-justifying thirst? Religious prestige will never satisfy your soul.

On what can you build your spiritual self-worth, if not your own social status? How about asking God to impart the worthiness of Jesus, so that your worth will depend on God's love for you, without regard to what anyone else thinks, in spite of the circumstances life brings?

If your self-worth is built on Jesus and his words and his love, then the specific seat you are assigned at a dinner is completely irrelevant. If your spiritual self-worth is built on Jesus—if he lives in you, then you will care less about your own esteem and prestige—far less about what others think and more about what Jesus thinks.

As I write, unemployment in many places here in North America is in double digits. People are suffering the financial hardship and humiliation of being unemployed. A friend of mine has been out of work almost two years, and he has been prayed for and encouraged by many friends. Yet a few "friends" have subtly removed him from their social calendar. Apparently the unemployed do not enhance the guest list.

The Lord does not play the exclusive guest list game, and those who love him do not abandon those who have been humbled by life's circumstances. The Lord exalts the humble and brings down the proud. Humility is the character of God. A slaughtered little lamb is the central symbol for Jesus in the Book of Revelation. All of heaven sings:

Revelation 5:12: "Worthy is the Lamb, who was slain, to receive power and wealth and wisdom and strength and honor and glory and praise!"

Jesus was exalted not because he seized exaltation, but because he relinquished it. He did not cling to his power and position. He emptied himself. He humbled himself. That is the character of God. As Paul wrote:

Philippians 2:5-11: "Your attitude should be the same as that of Christ Jesus: Who, being in very nature God, did not consider equality with God something to be grasped, but made himself nothing, taking the very nature of a servant, being made in human likeness. And being found in appearance as a man, he humbled himself and became obedient to death—even death on a cross! Therefore God exalted him to the highest place and gave him the name that is above every name, that at the name of Jesus every knee should bow, in heaven and on earth and under the earth, and every tongue confess that Jesus Christ is Lord, to the glory of God the Father."

By God's grace, our attitude can be that of Jesus, as he lives his risen life in us. Humility is one of the primary attributes of a Christ-centered life. When we are Christ-centered, Christ in us has no interest in being on the A-list, jockeying for position or seeking religious accolades and the praise of our fellows.

There is no wonder that religion leads to self-exaltation, because religion is all about human performance. What we do, when we do it and how much of it we accomplish are all the indicators which, institutionalized religion assures us, will adorn our heavenly scorecard. Heaven, as religion has it, is filled with angels who scurry around keeping score of our good deeds. By its very nature, Christ-less religion leads to competition, envy, greed and covetousness. Religion is all about human performance. Jesus is all about the humility he lives in us, by God's grace.

Jesus makes it crystal clear that the Pharisees were slaves of empty religion. They coveted the seats of honor at banquets. Their scorekeeping hearts made them jockey for positions of honor before their honor-hungry colleagues. How sad that rather than humbly serving the humble, they ignored the humble to exalt themselves.

God did not come to this earth, in the person of Jesus, so that we might serve him with peeled grapes, chocolate bars and ice cold drinks while fanning him with palm fronds. He came to serve us. While God desires our love and service, apart from his grace we have nothing he needs. He doesn't need any product we are capable of producing. What he desires is for us to accept his service, which will transform us from thinking solely of ourselves to being his very children who are humble, internally adorned with the attitude of Jesus, thinking of and serving others, in his name.

God is not interested in anything religion assures us that we can earn. Larger prayer phylacteries, longer prayer shawls and getting the places of honor at dining room tables earn you nothing before God. What matters to God is transforming us, by his grace, into his very children in whom Jesus lives.

Call No One Rabbi, Father or Teacher

Jesus was not finished with the Pharisees, the appearance-loving religious professionals. His next statement raises the question of what is appropriate, in God's eyes, to call religious professionals.

Rabbi, an Aramaic and Hebrew word, means "my great one," or "my honorable sir." It is most often translated as *Master*. It is a title of respect used when addressing a biblical expert. Jesus himself was addressed as *rabbi* frequently (Matthew 26:25, 49; Mark 9:5, 11:21, 14:45; John 1:38, 1:49, 3:2, 4:31, 6:25, 9:2), most often by his own disciples.

Jesus said, *"But you are not to be called 'Rabbi,' for you have only one Master and you are all brothers"* (Mathew 23:9). Humble as always, Jesus did not specify who this one Rabbi is. But we all know, since he allowed his disciples to address him as Rabbi. Moreover, Jesus equalizes everybody else. We are all brothers (and sisters).

Is Jesus telling us that we must not call a pastor or priest by honorary titles such as reverend, teacher, preacher, elder or bishop? Some religious professionals have advanced degrees. Is Jesus opposed to recognizing the title of doctor when we speak of or to a pastor?

Like phylacteries, tassels and chief seats in synagogues and at banquets, a title of honor is not a problem, in and of itself. Jesus is telling us to reserve the ultimate spiritual sense of what it means to be rabbi, father and teacher for God alone. There is no one-upmanship or competition for status if we are all equal, spiritual siblings. The religious game the Pharisees were playing was futile. Jesus exposes the lofty title game for what it really is: egotistical, arrogant, self-promoting snobbery. No one should fall for the idea that their title makes them a better or superior person. We should not think of those who have titles as being better or superior persons. When it comes to human beings, we are all in the same boat—we're humans. Jesus then goes a step further, and he steps right on our toes. He says the same thing about the title *father:*

Matthew 23:9: *"And do not call anyone on earth 'father,' for you have one Father, and he is in heaven."*

Jesus knew of the commandment to honor your father and your mother, of course. Obviously, he was not telling us to refrain from referring to our own fathers with the respectful title of "father." Jesus was not talking about the physical relationships we have, and the physical honor we owe

28

our parents. He was talking about the spiritual honor of father which our Father in heaven alone deserves.

Even at the age of twelve, Jesus said to his panicked mother and father, "'Why were you searching for me? …Didn't you know I had to be in my Father's house?'" (Luke 2:49) And when the grown Jesus was told that his mother and brothers were at the door, he told those gathered, "'Who are my mother and my brothers?' he asked. Then he looked at those seated in a circle around him and said, 'Here are my mother and my brothers! Whoever does God's will is my brother and sister and mother'" (Mark 3:33-35). Jesus used these occasions to intentionally distance himself from any claims of the ultimate priority of physical family in order to underline the eternal priority of spiritual family.

As with the title *rabbi*, Jesus limits the title *father*. Rabbi is a title appropriate only for God the Son. Father is a title appropriate only for God the Father. Jesus pulls the rug out from under anyone who would elevate himself, whether fathers or teachers of the law.

Then there is another title: *Teacher*. It is translated from a rare Greek word found only twice in the New Testament, both times in Matthew 23:10. The word is *kathegetes*, meaning "one who guides." Jesus not only calls the teachers of the law and Pharisees blind guides (Matthew 15:14, 23:16, 23:24), but he denied these blind guides the title of teacher. Jesus limited its spiritual and ultimate use to the Messiah (Paul uses a different Greek word for teacher in Ephesians 4:11).

Again, out of true humility, Jesus makes no claim here to being the Messiah, the Christ. He leaves that determination to his listeners. Talk about nerve! *Do not call anyone rabbi*, he says to religious leaders who covet the title. *Do not call anyone father*, he says to people who are proud of their religious observance of the commandments, including the one about honoring your parents. *Do not call anyone teacher*, he says to religious professionals who long to have others look to them as a spiritual guide and teacher.

Jesus gave these prohibitions because no mere mortal deserves these titles of honor, in their ultimate, spiritual sense. Those in whom Jesus lives, in all humility, will not covet such titles. *Humble yourselves and honor God alone.*

The Show of Religion in the Church

Are religious professionals today guilty of religion for show? Of course! Many religious authorities covet larger congregations and more beautiful buildings, bigger homes and cars, more respect in town and places of honor in the church and community, prestigious diplomas from better universities, higher offices in larger denominations, bigger salaries in churches with bigger budgets, best-selling books and large TV, radio and Internet audiences and ratings, and famous members from high places of commerce and government who attend their church.

Before we point fingers at religious leaders, however, we would all do well to check our own pride. Many people boast of their religious leaders as being better preachers. Others take pride in what they have been told is better theology, while still others bask in the spiritual arrogance of bigger denominations and nicer buildings. It's all religious pride. It's all a show. Christ-less religion is always about "the show." And therein is a huge red flag. If it's a show, can it be real and authentic? Think about it.

Our Prayer:
Father, Rabbi and Teacher: Apart from you we are all such posers and pretenders. Search us and reveal to us if our primary interest is in being image-conscious imposters. Expose our false façades, and lead us to the humble carpenter from Nazareth, whom we know, by your grace, as our King of kings, Lord of lords, Messiah and Savior.

30

Chapter 3

The Kingdom—The Cure for Religion

"Woe to you, teachers of the law and Pharisees, you hypocrites! You shut the kingdom of heaven in men's faces. You yourselves do not enter, nor will you let those enter who are trying to." —Matthew 23:13

This brief verse, **the first woe of Matthew 23**, is jam-packed with insight. What does *woe* mean? What does *hypocrite* mean? What is the *kingdom of heaven*? How does one enter the kingdom and how does one shut others out?

These are key New Testament concepts and questions critical to understanding Jesus' meaning. Let's unpack them.

Seven Woes!

Woe is not exactly an everyday word anymore, if it ever was. A definition is in order, since Jesus launches seven woes at religion and its leaders (Matthew 23:13, 15, 16, 23, 25, 27 and 29).

Woe is an *onomatopoeia* (a word whose sounds suggests the meaning it conveys). Words like *bang, woof* and *buzz* sound like the idea they represent. *Woe* does, too. *Woe* is a word which is a literal moan of grief.

Woe is a cry of deep despair that occurs 26 times in the Old Testament. *Woe* expresses horror and denunciation, and it is used to announce a disaster. Occurring 46 times in the New Testament, *woe* is a mournful exclamation of catastrophe.

In a way, when someone in the Bible says, "woe to you," a curse is being pronounced. But when Isaiah and Jeremiah and Jesus used this phrase, they were not saying, "I now curse you." They were saying, "You are cursed already because you are cursing yourself by what you are doing." Jesus did not come to curse (condemn) the world, but to save it from its cursed-ness.

"Woe to you" merely recognizes the choices of an individual, group or a nation—and the consequences of those choices. That's the way in which Jesus is using this word in context with religion. Religious legalism is a spiritual train wreck. The fact that Jesus says "woe to you" seven times in a row underlines the utter depths of his sorrow and outrage about the disastrous, catastrophic consequences of Christless religion.

Earlier in Jesus' ministry he stood and debated with the Pharisees. And throughout his ministry he managed to evade arrest and assault. But now at the end of his ministry he goes to Jerusalem to take a public stand against the religious leaders. Jesus' seven woes here in Matthew 23 mark and define the Judean religious leadership as a curse— because they were using their authority to dominate those they "served" rather than liberate them.

This is a life-or-death matter to Jesus—a matter worth dying for. He came to give life, and these religious leaders were dealing death. He called them "hypocrites," because they were not at all what they appeared to be. They shut the door to the kingdom of heaven, rather than opening it.

Jesus came to set the prisoners free, and the hypocritical religious leaders were the spiritual prison guards. They had turned his Father's house into a moneymaking scheme.

They had turned a house of prayer into a legalistic, religious system of domination. Speaking of the religious professionals, Jesus said:

Matthew 23:4: "They tie up heavy loads and put them on men's shoulders, but they themselves are not willing to lift a finger to move them."

The heavy loads are the regulations of the law. The Pharisees were sticklers. But why did they do this to people? If the religionists had really cared about the people that they served, they would not have merely enforced the law, but they would have shown them how to observe it. They would have shown them why it is important. But what did they do instead? They watched people for infractions and held their failures over their heads. Why? Power. Domination.

These religious professionals controlled people by subordinating and condemning them. They used the law to inflame the guilty and shamed consciences of those they "served." They were choking the life out of people with the law. Jesus showed these burdened, abused people another way. Jesus invites us all to drink of him, the living water, and experience the oasis of God's grace:

Matthew 11:28-30: "Come to me, all you who are weary and burdened, and I will give you rest. Take my yoke upon you and learn from me, for I am gentle and humble in heart, and you will find rest for your souls. For my yoke is easy and my burden is light."

By whom and what were these people burdened? They were weary of performance-based religion. They were oppressed by religion and its authorities. They were exhausted by nitpicking rules and regulations that were laid on their shoulders by religionists who, rather than sharing the burden, made it their business to dominate them by holding the club of legal condemnation over their heads. They were being yoked with an impossible load, and were being whipped for being unable to bear it.

33

This is not simply a historical example of religious oppression that ended, never to be seen or heard from again. Religion is alive and well, enslaving and oppressing people everywhere. Jesus offers rescue, relief and rest.

It's well been said that Jesus did not come to earth to start another religion. The world then, and now, has more than its fill of religion. Jesus didn't merely modify or remodel religion—he turned it upside down. Jesus offers us rest from the heavy-handed brutalities religion dishes out.

In the same way that Jesus was a threat to those religious lawyers and Pharisees then, he continues to represent an absolute revolutionary earthquake to the religious institutions of our day! If we listen carefully to Jesus, his teachings will reveal the evils of big-business religion! The gospel of the kingdom of God is an announcement that the time has come for religion to go out of business!

Religion and its authorities are obstacles to our relationship with God. Jesus makes it crystal clear. It's either him or religion. Accept his rest or live under the burden of religion.

Condemnations of Hypocrisy!

Just as Jesus organized this sermon around seven *woes*, he also adds six counts of hypocrisy to his indictment of the teachers of the law and the Pharisees—and the oppressive religion they represent.

We are using the New International Version (NIV) as our translation as we study Matthew 23. The NIV, along with most modern translations, omits verse 14, which is included in the authorized King James Version (KJV). Modern translators consider verse 14 to be an *interpolation*, a scribal addition found in later New Testament manuscripts, but not in the manuscripts of the early centuries. If you are reading the NIV you will find verse 14 included as a marginal footnote:

Matthew 23:14: *"Woe to you, teachers of the law and Pharisees,* *you hypocrites! You devour widows' houses and for a show make lengthy prayers. Therefore you will be punished more severely.*

While some find the significance of either six or seven references to "hypocrites" important (remember if you count verse 14 and make a case for seven instances of "hypocrites" then the "magic number" of woes moves from seven to eight!) the real significance here is not the precise number of iterations, but the sheer repetition.

Hypocrite is a Greek word that means "actor." Roman theaters had been constructed everywhere in the empire, including several in Israel, even in Jerusalem. Though theaters were considered unclean and off limits by many Jews, some Jews had a more relaxed perspective about acting and drama. Jews attended plays with their gentile neighbors in cities like Beit Shean, Tiberias, and Caesarea.

A Roman theater was excavated in a predominantly Jewish city called Sepphoris, located only four miles from Nazareth where Jesus grew up. Jesus' use of the word *hypocrite* comes from the context of Roman theaters, plays and the art of acting on a stage.

When Jesus called certain people hypocrites, he was calling them actors. Actors often played multiple roles in the same play by disguising themselves with different masks. The same actor might wear the mask of comedy, making the audience laugh, and then later in the same play switch to a mask of tragedy, delivering solemn, sad lines. Jesus may be referencing the Greek mask of tragedy when he said:

Matthew 6:16: *"When you fast, do not look somber as the hypocrites do, for they disfigure their faces to show men they are fasting. I tell you the truth, they have received their reward in full."*

Jesus is saying that religion is not what it appears to be. Its leadership and followers are not who they appear to be. They are masked. They are costumed. They are players on a stage. They are "two-faced"—imposing one standard on those they oppress while allowing themselves to behave in another manner altogether. Jesus said that the only reward these actors receive is that they get noticed.

Defining the Kingdom of Heaven

Whatever the kingdom of heaven is, it is no place for actors and charlatans. It is no place, therefore, for religion! The kingdom of heaven is a place of truth, an environment completely at odds with religious posers and pretenders. The Pharisees, the self-proclaimed purity police, were refusing to enter the kingdom, and were not allowing those to enter who wished to. So, biblically speaking, what is this kingdom of heaven?

Many today define the kingdom of heaven as a celestial place to which you go when you die. This is a strangely unbiblical definition. There are *four key features* that Jesus expresses about the kingdom of heaven.

First, Jesus says that the kingdom of heaven is present. Second, Jesus said that the kingdom of heaven is coming. Third, the kingdom of heaven is a mystery (hidden to human eyes) so Jesus uses everyday, down-to-earth objects like seeds, yeast and pearls to depict the kingdom. Fourth, Jesus defines the kingdom of heaven as eternal life.

So let's look at each of these four truths about the biblical kingdom of heaven. Let's look at the kingdom of heaven as present, as coming, as a hidden mystery revealed in parables and as eternal life.

First, the kingdom of heaven Jesus proclaimed is present:

Matthew 3:2: "Repent, for the kingdom of heaven is near."
Matthew 4:17: "From that time on Jesus began to preach, 'Repent, for the kingdom of heaven is near.'"
Matthew 10:7: "As you go, preach this message: 'The kingdom of heaven is near.'"

Legalistic religion loves to use the word "repent" as a device to convince its followers to get with its program.

The message is the same, across-the-board in legalistic churches: "Stop doing the stuff you are doing and start doing what we want you to do." Religion is all about do-do-do. It truly is a huge pile of do-do.

But the word translated as repent, *metanoeo*, literally means to change your mind. Change your mind about what? Change your mind that God is far off. He is near. His presence is not bad news. Change your mind. Reject religion; embrace God. God's presence is bad news for religion's prison-economy, and all the people who work to keep people enslaved—but it's great news for the inmates!

Jesus' presence is the essence of the kingdom of heaven (or of God). His power is kingdom power. His good news is kingdom news.

Luke 17:20-21: "Once, having been asked by the Pharisees when the kingdom of God would come, Jesus replied, 'The kingdom of God does not come with your careful observation, nor will people say, 'Here it is,' or 'There it is,' because the kingdom of God is within you.'"

His presence is its presence. To speak of the kingdom of heaven biblically is not to speak of a far away place that you merely go to when you die. In Scripture, it is God's present relational reality and realm, present now even as he is present forever:

Matthew 28:20: "And surely I am with you always, to the very end of the age."

Jesus is present always, and therefore his kingdom is present always. He is all in all. He is the one in whom all people live and move and have their being (Acts 17:28). His kingdom is not *of* this world (John 18:36), but it encompasses this world, and it is surely *in* this world as he is always with us in this world. Jesus makes the presence of his kingdom of heaven real in these promises:

Matthew 5:3: "Blessed are the poor in spirit, for theirs is the kingdom of heaven."

Matthew 5:10: "Blessed are those who are persecuted because of righteousness, for theirs is the kingdom of heaven."
Matthew 19:14: "Jesus said, 'Let the little children come to me, and do not hinder them, for the kingdom of heaven belongs to such as these.'"

Notice that Jesus uses the present tense. The poor in spirit, the persecuted, the children who come to Jesus possess the kingdom of heaven *now*. It is theirs. It belongs to them. They are living in it.

But note that those who are powerless and disenfranchised do not earn the kingdom of heaven. They are simply said to have it, not by virtue of virtuous living, but by virtue of the fact that they admit their innate spiritual poverty, while accepting the riches of God's grace, given without human cause or divine reservation.

The kingdom of heaven is not mediated or bartered or delivered through religious intermediaries. The kingdom of heaven is a direct, one-on-one relationship, freely available to all, regardless of educational or religious qualifications, age, gender, culture, creed or race. You may have served time in a cult, as I did, and while that fact may mean you are suspect to "respectable" religion, you are more than welcome in the kingdom of heaven.

Relationship is about knowing and being known. The kingdom of heaven is real life—the very life of the risen Lord, Jesus Christ of Nazareth. The kingdom of heaven is eternal life, the gift of God, by grace. Eternal life is knowing God the Father and God the Son (John 17:3).

Part of what it means to be created in God's image (Genesis 1:27) is that created humans yearn for connection with the Creator God. We are incomplete—we are missing something—if we do not connect with God. Religion enters the picture as a counterfeit, knock-off spiritual relationship. It deceives and lies, presenting its customs, traditions, regulations and ceremonies as a direct line to heaven if and when we will march to its drumbeat. But God doesn't need religious middle-men.

While there are truly authentic, Christ-centered teachers, pastors and authors (I am blessed to know many, and of course there are far more whom I do not know personally) there are also religious middle-men who are scam artists, actors, frauds and slave drivers. That's the unequivocal message of Matthew 23!

Let's turn our attention back to the kingdom of heaven. The kingdom of heaven is an open, intimate, close, no-secrets relationship with God. We experience God's peace and his presence (as opposed to our guilt and shame exploited by religion) when we know and are known by God, openly, honestly and unguardedly.

Time and time again in the Gospels we read of Jesus either attending a wedding feast, a banquet or a party of some nature—or speaking of doing so in one of his parables. Jesus loved parties—he still does! The kingdom of heaven is a true, spiritual celebration—the kingdom of heaven is a present tense, ongoing celebration of knowing and being known in complete and utter freedom and truth.

The kingdom of heaven is eternal joy. It is an ever-present life-party that defeats fear and brings faith, hope and love into any dark circumstance.

Second, although the kingdom of heaven is ever-present, it is also ever-coming.

Matthew 6:9-10: "This, then, is how you should pray: 'Our Father in heaven, hallowed be your name, your kingdom come...'"

Your kingdom come. Jesus clearly insists that the kingdom of heaven (the kingdom of God is, of course, one and the same as the kingdom of heaven) has already come, as well as teaching that it has not yet fully arrived. We can see it and live in it now, but it will not be here in its fullness until the last day when he returns, as Jesus said poetically, on the clouds of heaven (Matthew 26:64; Mark 14:62).

The kingdom of heaven has all three dimensions in human time—it is past—it is present, alive and active in our world today, available to you and me—and it has a future, grand culmination in glory. *The kingdom of heaven is already but not yet.*

It's important to note here that while most in Christendom speak of "going to heaven when you die," Jesus spoke about living in the kingdom of heaven now and forever. And, strange but true, he did not specifically speak of "going to" heaven after we die. He said that the kingdom is coming to you in its fullness on the last day. *Thy kingdom come.*

So, paradoxically, the kingdom of heaven is both present and coming. We are invited to see it now, seek it now, enter it now and live in it now. But we are also told to pray for its final coming in fullness. As we now see Jesus indirectly, we can now only see the kingdom indirectly, as but a poor reflection in a mirror (1 Corinthians 13:12). But on the last day we will see him face to face, and therefore we will also then perceive and experience his kingdom in all its fullness.

Third, the kingdom of heaven is a mystery—hidden to human eyes. Jesus was clear about this hidden character of the kingdom of heaven. So he explained the kingdom in a hidden way. He revealed the mystery that is the presence of the kingdom of heaven in the mystery of parables. Here are three examples:

Matthew 13:33: *"He told them still another parable: 'The kingdom of heaven is like yeast that a woman took and mixed into a large amount of flour until it worked all through the dough.'"*
Matthew 13:44: *"The kingdom of heaven is like treasure hidden in a field. When a man found it, he hid it again, and then in his joy went and sold all he had and bought that field."*
Matthew 13:45-46: *"Again, the kingdom of heaven is like a merchant looking for fine pearls. When he found one of great value, he went away and sold everything he had and bought it."*

The mystery that is the kingdom of heaven is like the pinch of living yeast that causes the whole batch of dough to rise. It is the living joy that makes a man liquidate everything to buy a field with a secret buried treasure. It is the urgency of a pearl merchant who stumbles across the pearl of all pearls, joyfully selling his entire stock to buy that precious one.

Too many times these parables are preached through the distorted lens of religious duty and obligation—whereby the kingdom is achieved through human effort. Christ-less religion tells us that we have to add *Jesus-yeast* to our lives—read our Bibles and pray every day. We are told we must join and attend ("go to") church and tithe if we want to get the treasure.

Performance-based sermons tell us that we have to give up everything we love in order to get the pearl of salvation, when in fact the parable actually describes Jesus selling everything he had and purchasing you and me (after all, how in the world can we afford to buy Jesus?).

Where, in Jesus' teaching, is the idea of earning or purchasing or gaining the kingdom of heaven or being rewarded with it, based on our religious performance? Where does Jesus stipulate the number of rituals one must perform, how many laws one must obey, how many candles one must light to gain the kingdom of heaven? Where did the idea come from that we must qualify, or "make it" into the kingdom of heaven based on our performance?

When you hear about a kingdom that you can gain or attain on the basis of your performance, be forewarned—the kingdom being promoted is a part of the kingdom of religion. Gaining God's kingdom of heaven by virtue of our virtues? Are you kidding me?

The parables of Jesus never attempt to guilt us into dutiful drudgery. Jesus gave parables about the mystery, presence and value of the kingdom of heaven. But he did not stop there. He also explained how God imparts his kingdom:

41

Matthew 5:20: *"For I tell you that unless your righteousness surpasses that of the Pharisees and the teachers of the law, you will certainly not enter the kingdom of heaven."*
Matthew 7:21: *"Not everyone who says to me, 'Lord, Lord,' will enter the kingdom of heaven, but only he who does the will of my Father who is in heaven."*
Matthew 18:3: *"And he said: 'I tell you the truth, unless you change and become like little children, you will never enter the kingdom of heaven.'"*

These three quotes impart three important truths about entering the kingdom of heaven:

• *Unless your righteousness surpasses that of the Pharisees and the teachers of the law, you will certainly not enter the kingdom of heaven.* How can your righteousness surpass that of the meticulously observant Pharisees and lawyers? It cannot, and that is Jesus' point. If you define righteousness as your high score at keeping the law, as did the Pharisees, you will fail. But by God's grace you can be transformed from what you were to what he enables you to be—completely righteous (2 Corinthians 5:21). God gives us his righteousness, apart from law, which comes "through faith in Jesus Christ to all who believe" (Romans 3:21-22).

• *Not all who say "Lord, Lord" will enter the kingdom of heaven.* Anyone can sound religious. All you have to do is sprinkle your vocabulary with theological words. You can go around quoting Scripture and praying in Jesus' name. But if Jesus is not producing God's love in and through you, you are not a part of the kingdom of heaven. God's kingdom is a kingdom of love. Love is God's will. Those who love as God loves do so because that love is given to them by God's grace and lived in them through the risen Jesus Christ (1 John 4:7-12). Those who belong to the kingdom of heaven are doing the will of God because they are one in Christ, and it is Jesus who works in them to produce the will of God.

- *Unless you change and become like little children, you will never enter the kingdom of heaven.* What are little children like? Without money, without knowledge and wisdom, they simply live in trust that they are loved and cared for. They realize and accept their dependence on their parents. Little children do not question provision. Religious striving is not even on their radar. They just toddle over to Mama and crawl into her lap, safe and secure. People who are spiritually re-born, born from above (John 3:3), transformed by God's grace, born not of natural descent or human decision, but of God's grace (John 1:13) have entered the kingdom of heaven.

Think again about the signature verse for this chapter:

Matthew 23:13: "Woe to you, teachers of the law and Pharisees, you hypocrites! You shut the kingdom of heaven in men's faces. You yourselves do not enter, nor will you let those enter who are trying to."

Fourth, Jesus defined the kingdom of heaven as eternal life. In Matthew's Gospel it is most often called the kingdom of heaven. In Mark and Luke's Gospels, it is usually called the kingdom of God. But in John's Gospel, it is called life, abundant life, or eternal life. To enter the kingdom is to enter life. So what is life in the kingdom of heaven?

John 17:3: "Now this is eternal life: that they may know you, the only true God, and Jesus Christ, whom you have sent."

The kingdom of heaven/the kingdom of God is a relationship—an eternal, living, relational reality. To know the one who is the way, the truth and the life is to know the kingdom of heaven. And people who live in the kingdom are people who love because God empowers them, by his grace, through Jesus Christ, to do so.

Citizens of the kingdom of heaven love in spite of the fact that they know they are sinners. They love in spite of the fact that they tend to lapse into trying to prove their own righteousness through religious striving.

By knowing God the Father and God the Son, citizens of the kingdom of heaven know and experience a kingdom of grace. And by trusting and resting in that grace like a toddler in his mother's lap, they find real freedom, real joy, real peace and real life. Free from the heavy burden of religious striving, free from the condemnation of sin, free from the domination of religious taskmasters, free from pompous posing, those who accept the kingdom of heaven, by God's grace, are free indeed.

John 8:36: "So if the Son sets you free, you will be free indeed."

Those who pose and pretend are evidencing their lack of trust in the kingdom of heaven's grace to sinners. And, if the truth be told, sometimes the posers and pretenders are you and me. But grace covers the sins of posing and pretending, too. Paul also defined the kingdom:

Romans 14:17: For the kingdom of God is not a matter of eating and drinking, but of righteousness, peace and joy in the Holy Spirit...

Virtually all of Paul's letters deal with problems concerning practice and behavior. He normally explains a specific theological foundation of the kingdom of heaven and then illustrates that foundation with practical ways that Jesus lives out the theology of the kingdom of heaven in those who live in him.

In Romans 14 Paul addresses the question: Do Christians have to follow Jewish dietary laws? Must gentile Christians start keeping kosher? Can Jewish Christians drop their kosher diets?

Should Christians buy meat in the markets of their cities knowing that some of the meat came from sacrificial rites in pagan temples? How much should be eaten and drunk at the Lord's Supper—a whole meal or a bite, a sip of wine or a glass or two?

Paul had to deal with dietary problems repeatedly in the churches he served, and his concern about religious attention to food and drink is that it becomes just so much more religious striving, and it misses the main point of their faith in Jesus' righteousness. Righteousness in the New Testament is "right relatedness."

Jesus makes us rightly related to the Father and one another. Right relationship with God transcends squabbles and rules about food and drink. Your relationship to the Father through the Son in the Holy Spirit produces rest, trust and the fruits of peace and joy. That is the kingdom of heaven (of God), says Paul. Do not let worry over food or anything else get in the way of that.

Matthew 6:31-34: "So do not worry, saying, 'What shall we eat?' or 'What shall we drink?' or 'What shall we wear?' For the pagans run after all these things, and your heavenly Father knows that you need them. But seek first his kingdom and his righteousness, and all these things will be given to you as well. Therefore do not worry about tomorrow, for tomorrow will worry about itself. Each day has enough trouble of its own."

The Kingdom of Heaven or the Kingdom of Religion?

I was once a card-carrying member of a cult. I bought into the teachings of Herbert W. Armstrong (the collective body of these teachings today is often called *Armstrongism*) hook, line and sinker. I was a true believer. It's fascinating to see the reactions of people when I tell them I was once in a cult. If I'm talking with a group of people and the subject comes up, it's as if all the air has suddenly been sucked out of the room. Everyone gets really quiet, while they anticipate me telling lurid stories about how I once sacrificed goats and defaced cemeteries. Polite society, especially "good, church-going folks" tend to regard someone who is an ex-cult member as being roughly equivalent to an ex-convict. The typical, usually unstated reaction is something like, "How could you have been so stupid?"

There is no doubt about it—I was a sucker. I bought into a spiritual snow-job. Armstrongism seemed so plausible, because it was based on my ability to make God happy. Of course, I believed what I wanted to believe. I believed I had the spiritual power to please God. According to Armstrong in-speak, I could "qualify" for the kingdom of God. I could "make it" if I built enough "holy, righteous character."

Armstrongism appealed to my vanity, because I was told that the vast majority of people didn't "have the truth" like I did (in retrospect, I can only say "thank God" they didn't!). It was a religion, in that it filled me with fear of God's punishment if I failed to measure up. Like any and all religions, my experience with cultic religion manipulated my guilt and shame. I didn't know it at the time, but Armstrongism "shut the kingdom of heaven" in my face (Matthew 23:13).

Cultic religion (and all religion for that matter) exercises control over your life with long lists of rules, accompanied by the punishments exacted and the shame doled out when you are unable to measure up to those rules. Religion, whether it is deemed by culture to be acceptable or unacceptable, is all about human performance and how that performance is presumed to please and appease God.

Rules of Armstrongism included no pork or shellfish. No Christmas or Easter. No cosmetics for women. No "worldly" friends. No celebration of birthdays. No voting or service on a jury. No dating or marriage of anyone who was an "outsider." No involvement in politics. No participation in work or sports from sundown on Friday until sundown on Saturday (Saturday was the "true" sabbath). "Holy" days, as stipulated in the Old Testament, replaced what were called "falsely-so-called" Christian holidays.

Given my experiences, and most importantly, my rescue, by God's grace, I have come to know many thousands of spiritual refugees, people whom Christ-less religion has chewed up and spit out. It is my privilege to minister to those who, in some way, were once duped and deceived by religion.

The people I serve come from virtually every major religious institution broadly represented by the world of Christendom. They are spiritual refugees from religious bondage and exploitation at the hands of "respectable" churches as well as that inflicted by the world of the cults.

When spiritual refugees tell me their sad tales of grief and misery suffered at the hands of Christ-less religion, they often look back and realize they were hoodwinked by some spiritual snow-job or spiritual hoax.

As I have served those who have had similar experiences in widely divergent religious groups, I have come to see that all religion, whether deemed to be a cult or not, is a con. The kingdom of religion seems so right, so virtuous and so noble.

Religion appeals to our human desire to be able to control our own spiritual destinies, to manipulate God into loving us on the basis of our performance.

The kingdom of religion appeals to human vanity, telling us that what we know and what we do makes us better than others who are not part of our religious club. Legalistic religion threatens its followers with fear of the punishment they will surely endure if they fail to fall into line. Religion preys on our guilt and shame, assuring us we can make God happy if we work hard enough. Human performance is the common denominator upon which all religious cons base their empty claims and promises.

Generally speaking, the well-known world religions subscribed to and believed by hundreds of millions of people are felt to be harmless. The reasoning goes something like this: "How could hundreds of millions of people be deceived—and if their religion is hurting them in some way, then why don't they just leave? How could hundreds of millions of people buy into a con?"

There was a time when the world of Christendom at large felt that Mormonism was a cult. But now, given the political and economic influence arising out of the sheer numbers of Mormons, the Church of Jesus Christ of Latter Day Saints is now often respectfully called a religion or a denomination. It goes without saying that Mormons are not fond of being called a "cult" and do all they can to avoid that label.

There is no question that there is a need to expose cults that attempt to pass themselves off as Christian, for they are toxic counterfeits.

• **Cults masquerade as being authentic** and orthodox, in their teaching and practice.

• **Cults are a sham**, they are dangerous and they are definitely a toxic hazard to spiritual health!

• **Cults** that operate behind the skirts of authentic Christianity **reject sound, historically-validated biblical teaching, beginning with how they understand the nature of God.**

• **Cults reject biblical accountability,** often leading their followers into dysfunctional, even bizarre religious practices.

• **Cults reject the centrality of Jesus Christ**, in favor of some form of performance-based legalism, which in turn often leads to abuse, in the name of God.

But in its zeal to reveal the inherent perils of cultic teaching, the more orthodox, "time-honored" big-business religion often neglects to subject itself to its own spiritual examination. Religious institutions and their members often kid themselves that they are immune from harmful practices and teaching by virtue of their longevity and their size. By this rationale, the early New Testament Christian church was a cult, because, compared with other religious movements, it had only just begun and it was small in numbers.

One of my favorite quotes from George Bernard Shaw goes something like this: "If 50 million people [the estimated population of Great Britain when Shaw originally penned the words] say or do a stupid thing it's still a stupid thing."

In an effort to preserve their own reputations, established religions enshrine themselves and their beliefs as being acceptable, taking pride in their crusades to condemn small, new, emerging movements. They proclaim those who march to their drumbeat to be legitimate—while those who don't are maligned as illegitimate.

Sometimes it actually is a case of the pot calling the kettle black (the practice of accusing another of faults that one has themselves)! Religious institutions, some of which amount to corporate empires, pride themselves on their political clout and number of constituents, and find fault with the speck of sawdust in other's eyes, without considering the huge plank in their own (Matthew 7:3-5).

One of the meanings given for the word "cult" by the Oxford English Dictionary is remarkably the same as I believe applies to the world of religion at large: "A particular form or system of religious worship; especially in reference to its external rites and ceremonies." You may have heard some of the jokes about popular definitions of the word "cult"—"anyone who doesn't agree with me" or "the church that I don't attend."

The primary meaning of both "cult" and "religion" are virtually one and the same—"a system of religious beliefs, practices, observances and rituals through which humans are persuaded they may appease and please God." In the broadest sense, all religions are cults. Initially, as I left the world of cultic teaching and practice, I thought that almost any respected church would be based on God's grace, and centered in and on Jesus Christ. Another shock!

Within a few years of my miraculous rescue from Armstrongism, by God's grace, I found out that legalistic teachings and practices are not confined to groups generally accepted as cults. The more I came to know the Jesus I never knew, and the more he transformed me, the less religious I became.

Today, I describe myself as an irreligious Christian—
a relationship I believe to be absolutely necessary, given
religion's hold on the world of Christendom.

Woes, Hypocrites and the Kingdom of Heaven

Woe is a bemoaning of a catastrophe. *Hypocrite* means one
who wears the mask and costume of an actor on the stage.
So what is the hypocritical catastrophe? Jesus says that
legalistic, authoritarian religious professionals are not entering the kingdom of heaven and are slamming the door in
the faces of those who try.

Jesus chided religious professionals who were merely
playing a role, memorizing the script that religion had
assigned them. Jesus compared empty, Christ-less religion
and its leading characters as a theater with performers bent
on performance.

Jesus clearly and concisely explains that legalistic religion at large believes that God's relationship with any human
being is based on how well that person performs works of
the law.

Religious professionals, then and now, put on a good
show (watch what passes for Christianity on television and
you'll see what Jesus means!). Religious professionals, actors
that they are, tell people that the only way people can please
God is to imitate their hypocritical behavior. Put on a religious show, they say. To that lie, Jesus cries, *Woe to you, you
hypocrites!*

While living in the hell that religion devises and enforces,
legalistic, oppressive religious actors and slave drivers
seduce people into entering religious hell with them.

Striving that thrives in the kingdom of religion cannot
exist in the kingdom of heaven any more than darkness can
exist in light. Light swallows up darkness. The kingdom of
heaven swallows up, blots out and will eventually put all
religious oppression and legalism out of business.

Our Prayer:
Lord, we are woeful hypocrites bent on our own way, obsessed with appearance and status, determined to justify ourselves before you. Our attempts to impress you and others by putting on a religious show are fake, empty, hollow lies. Apart from you we are helplessly trapped in a variety of cultic, religious swamps. Help us every day to face the truth about ourselves. Lead us every day to the joy and peace that comes from fully embracing Jesus, fully experiencing you as our only hope, our only righteousness, given to us in your grace-filled, freedom-filled, kingdom of heaven. Renew us and shape us day by day, by your grace. May your kingdom come, now and forever.

Chapter 4

The Hell of It All

"Woe to you, teachers of the law and Pharisees, you hypocrites! You travel over land and sea to win a single convert, and when he becomes one, you make him twice as much a son of hell as you are."
—Matthew 23:15

uthor C.S. Lewis tells a story about a young boy's first encounter with a pastoral religious authority. At first, the pastor seems to be a warm, engaging person—initially their discussion centers around fishing and bicycles. But then, without warning, the pastor takes a terrifying mask with a long white beard off the wall of his office. The pastor puts the mask on his face and tells the young boy, named John, he is now going to talk to him about God. He then assures John that God is very kind, but if John doesn't obey all the rules God will shut him up forever in a black hole full of snakes and scorpions (C.S. Lewis, *The Pilgrim's Regress*).

Religion provides lurid details about hell, and dogmatically insists that God will condemn those who don't measure up to eternal torture. Jesus talks about hell, but the hell Jesus talks about in this **second woe of Matthew 23** is a place where the religious leaders reside. The hell to which Jesus has reference in our signature passage is a place for which religion recruits. As we will see, this hell Jesus speaks of is anti-grace, anti-freedom and anti-kingdom of heaven.

Ironic, isn't it? Christ-less religion places a great deal of emphasis on how it can help you stay out of hell, but Jesus says that religious professionals are actually luring you into hell. In a nutshell, Jesus is saying that the teachers of the law and Pharisees are *the damned leading others into damnation.*

Following the teaching Jesus gave in the signature verse for this chapter, let's examine what Jesus has to say about 1) religious authorities and leaders, 2) the hell of religion, 3) evangelistic techniques religion uses to lure the unsuspecting and 4) the spiritual freedom Jesus offers, as opposed to the lifestyles of churchianity.

Teachers of the Law

Teachers of the law, called "scribes" in the Authorized King James Version, were highly educated, top-flight scholars whose life's work was expert knowledge and interpretation of the biblical law. They considered themselves to be the true teachers of the people. The people, however, were impressed with Jesus' teaching because he did not teach like the scribes.

Matthew 7:28-29: *"When Jesus had finished saying these things, the crowds were amazed at his teaching, because he taught as one who had authority, and not as their teachers of the law.*

Teachers of the law appealed to the authority of others. They referenced what Moses said and what former rabbis at the temple said, like Rabbi Hillel and Rabbi Shammai. So when someone asked a question, a teacher of the law might explain the answers previously spoken by Moses and great teachers of the past, and how those various answers may not agree. But that was beside the point. Their job was to list the options and expound on them. Expect a long, detailed exposition from a teacher of the law. But do not expect a definitive answer.

Unlike the teachers of the law, Jesus gave colorful, incisive, inspiring and definitive answers. That is what the people meant when they said Jesus spoke with authority. He did not reference half-a-dozen rabbis, brilliantly juggling their complex and sometimes conflicting answers. Instead of obscuring an answer in scholarship, Jesus pulled the trigger and shot straight.

When he was asked a question, his response did not rely on past legal decisions made by deceased rabbis, because Jesus' authority was not based on dead men. He spoke with the authority of eternity because he was God in the flesh.

For example, consider a few of Jesus' teachings within what is popularly called the Sermon on the Mount:

Matthew 6:24: *"No one can serve two masters. Either he will hate the one and love the other, or he will be devoted to the one and despise the other. You cannot serve both God and Money."*

Matthew 6:34: *"Therefore do not worry about tomorrow, for tomorrow will worry about itself. Each day has enough trouble of its own."*

Matthew 7:3: *"Why do you look at the speck of sawdust in your brother's eye and pay no attention to the plank in your own eye?"*

Matthew 7:7: *"Ask and it will be given to you; seek and you will find; knock and the door will be opened to you."*

There is no theological juggling going on here. Jesus speaks with authority. He does not speak like someone who hasn't been able to recover from the high-sounding, intellectual philosophy and theology he heard in seminary. Jesus doesn't cite erudite, impossible-to-understand theologians as his authority. He speaks and teaches using ordinary language, employing examples from everyday life.

Of course, this very attribute made Jesus popular, and this very attribute made the religious leaders hate him. They hated the fact that Jesus had not been trained by their religious authorities, and they hated the fact that Jesus' style of teaching was popular and appreciated by the people at large. Jesus was making the religious leaders look bad, so obviously, they wanted to get rid of him.

Some pastors, priests, ministers and ministry leaders seem to be unable (or perhaps unwilling, I don't know) to simply preach and teach Jesus. It may sound somewhat simple, but it seems to me if we are ministers of Jesus Christ then we appeal to his authority, and we proclaim him.

The mere attribution or citation of theologians and scholars, when they help bring clarity to the gospel can be helpful, but I am thinking of those who endlessly go on and on about their favorite theologian. My favorite theologian is Jesus. There are many grace-based, Christ-centered pastors, priests, scholars and authors—men and women from whom I have learned much. But my favorite theologian and my favorite author is Jesus. My next favorite theologians and authors are those who speak endlessly of Jesus and who are relentlessly Christ-centered!

Matthew 13:52: *"He said to them, 'Therefore every teacher of the law who has been instructed about the kingdom of heaven is like the owner of a house who brings out of his storeroom new treasures as well as old.'"*

When Jesus gave this parable, the "old" was the traditions of Old Testament Judaism up to and through the time of John the Baptist. The "new" was the revelation of Jesus Christ, the in-the-flesh presence of the Word of God in the world, and therefore the presence of the kingdom of heaven. To understand better what Jesus means by old and new, consider his parable about old and new wineskins.

Mark 2:22: "And no one pours new wine into old wineskins. If he does, the wine will burst the skins, and both the wine and the wineskins will be ruined. No, he pours new wine into new wineskins." (See also Matthew 9:17 and Luke 5:37-38).

To understand Jesus' teachings (new wine) you need to accept the spiritual reality that, in Jesus, God is present in a new way. You need God to renew and transform your mind (Romans 12:2), so that your mind will be a new mind (wineskin) for his new wine. The presence of Jesus, God in the flesh, is the presence of the kingdom of heaven (or God), and that kingdom is at work revealing a new teaching (wine). Jesus is the fulfillment of the Old Testament law and prophets, and he fulfills them in humble service and suffering. The old wineskins of "old time religion" cannot contain Jesus' teachings.

Jesus used this wineskin parable to illustrate why the religious authorities were not "getting it." Their brains were bursting because their brains were programmed by religion! Their old religious framework was not sufficient to contain the new work that God was doing in Jesus. His message was blowing their minds then, just as it continues to do now, when the dynamic, life-giving wine of his gospel encounters tired religious traditions and rituals.

Pharisees

When introducing myself to an audience that does not know me I often adapt the phrase customarily used in Alcoholics Anonymous—except I apply it to *Not So Anonymous Legalists*. "Hi, I'm Greg, and I'm a religious legalist." Of course, by God's grace, much of my legalism is in the past. However, I never want to be so naïve as to think that legalism can never get its grimy tentacles on me again.

I am, by God's grace, a recovering legalist. I have legalistic scars. I am as susceptible to religious legalism as a recovering alcoholic is to wine. Given the ever-present danger of legalism, my goal is to be an irreligious Christian. We who have made the journey from religion to Jesus realize that such a spiritual journey is possible because "nothing is impossible with God" (Luke 1:37).

Rejecting legalism and accepting Jesus can only be accomplished by God's grace, as Jesus lives his life in us, empowering us to rest in Christ, in spite of all of the religious instruction, training and brainwashing to which we have been subjected. And remember—individuals, whether followers or religious leaders, are deceived and victimized by religious culture, tradition and methodology. The real culprit is legalistic, Christ-less religion!

As we carefully examine the Gospels we see that the Pharisees, more than any group of religious professionals of that day, were constantly on Jesus' case. The Gospels reveal that it was the Pharisees at large who monitored him, challenged him, harassed him, condemned him, had him arrested and eventually put to death. Their problems with him were, predictably, over matters of the law.

The Pharisees often objected to Jesus' lack of obedience to their traditions and regulations. Jesus and his disciples did not perform the hand-washing ritual, so the Pharisees complained (Matthew 15:2). The Pharisees were upset because Jesus' disciples did not fast as they did (Matthew 9:14-15; Mark 2:18; Luke 5:33) and that he ate with sinners (Matthew 9:11; Mark 2:16; Luke 5:30).

But of all their objections to Jesus' behavior, their most frequent accusation against Jesus was that he was a Sabbath breaker. Jesus' disciples plucked heads of grain to eat on the Sabbath (Matthew 12:1-8; Mark 2:23-28; Luke 6:1-5), which was considered by the Pharisees to be work. Work was prohibited on the Sabbath. The Pharisees' most frequent complaint about Jesus was that he healed on the Sabbath, which was also considered work, and when they combined this affront with Jesus' blasphemous claim that God was "his own father" they determined to kill him (John 5:18). Religion is not happy when its traditions and authority are questioned!

Mark 3:4-5: "Then Jesus asked them, 'Which is lawful on the Sabbath: to do good or to do evil, to save life or to kill?' But they remained silent. He looked around at them in anger and, deeply distressed at their stubborn hearts..."

The Pharisees are the Bible's "exhibit A" of religious legalism. The Pharisees truly believed that their relationship with God depended on their ability to obey and keep commandments, laws, rules and regulations. By opposing Jesus they were opposing the kingdom of heaven (of God). They would not enter its grace and freedom and rest, and they hindered others from entering. The Pharisees, and religious legalists at large, rejected the kingdom of heaven in favor of a religious kingdom Jesus called hell. They not only lived in a spiritual kingdom of hell but they attempted to lure others into the same spiritual bondage they were enduring.

Gehenna—the Hell of Religion

The word *Gehenna* occurs only a dozen times in the New Testament. The term has reference to the Valley of Hinnom. You can visit hell when you visit Jerusalem today—it's downhill from the southern wall of the Old City of Jerusalem. The valley was notorious for two things:

First, children were sacrificed to Molech there. While there is some disagreement about all of the details, the traditional view is that Molech was an idol to whom the Ammonites in particular burned and sacrificed their children.

Kings Ahaz and Manasseh, in accommodation to local pagan rituals, reintroduced "children passing through the fire to Molech," probably child sacrifice (2 Kings 16:3; 2 Chronicles 28:3, 33:6; Jeremiah 7:30-34; 19:2-6). The Valley of Hinnom was called Topheth which means "place of fire." King Josiah outlawed the idolatrous and barbaric practice, (2 Kings 23:10) though it was already outlawed in Israel's legal code:

Leviticus 18:21: "Do not give any of your children to be sacrificed to Molech, for you must not profane the name of your God. I am the LORD."

Second, the valley, defiled by idolatrous human sacrifices, became a receptacle of animal carcasses and criminals' corpses for the city of Jerusalem. The Hinnom Valley (Gehenna) became Jerusalem's ever-burning garbage dump and sewer. It was the garbage dump for practical reasons, because all waste in Jerusalem flowed away from the city into the valley. It was a burning garbage dump, complete with all of the toxins and unpleasant odors of a dump, and no one lived there. The Hebrews made the place their sewer, their dump and their body disposal site. In Old and New Testament times, the fires of Gehenna reportedly never went out.

Hinnom in the Old Testament occurs only eleven times

in eleven verses, none of them in reference to anything other than the literal Hinnom Valley of south Jerusalem. (Joshua 15:8; Joshua 18:16; 2 Kings 23:10; 2 Chronicles 28:3; 2 Chronicles 33:6; Nehemiah 11:30; Jeremiah 7:31, 32; Jeremiah 19:2, 6; Jeremiah 32:35). None of these eleven references to the valley is used as a metaphor for the afterlife.

Welcome to the Gehenna of the New Testament, the valley of burning sewage and garbage and corpses that represents the ever-present danger of spiritual death. There is a "Death Valley" in the state of California, but Gehenna is the spiritual Death Valley. This Gehenna is not just in Jerusalem. This Gehenna is all around us. We live in the stench of it every day. You need more proof of its presence? Look again at this chapter's signature verse:

Matthew 23:15: "Woe to you, teachers of the law and Pharisees, you hypocrites! You travel over land and sea to win a single convert, and when he becomes one, you make him twice as much a son of hell [Gehenna] *as you are."*

Look at this verse, which we discuss in Chapter Eight:

Matthew 23:33: "You snakes! You brood of vipers! How will you escape being condemned to hell [Gehenna]*?"*

Notice Jesus says that the teachers of the law and Pharisees are *already* children of hell. Gehenna tragically defines whose they are and where they are from. They come from hell, they are in hell and they belong to hell. Gehenna is a spiritual toxin that resides in their soul. They cannot run from it, because Gehenna is inside them.

The teachers of the law and Pharisees are in a spiritual Death Valley, and it is in them. They have applied judgment to themselves by judging others. If they try to flee the judgment by hypocritically acting, appearing "holy" to others, they take the filth of Gehenna with them.

Is Jesus saying that the teachers of the law and Pharisees are literally snakes (Matthew 23:33)? Is he saying that they are literally whitewashed tombs, gleaming on the outside but full of dead men's bones and putrefaction (Matthew 23:27)? Obviously not.

Then is Jesus saying that hypocrites will be thrown into the literal burning dump in the Hinnom Valley (Gehenna)? By the same token, obviously not. If someone is already in a pit or swamp, you cannot throw them in. The teachers of the law, according to Jesus, were *already in hell*—a perfect image describing their true spiritual condition.

Many fail to adequately and accurately appreciate the extent to which Jesus used poetic pictures in his teaching. Jesus salted his teaching with parabolic images, sounds, tastes, smells and textures. For him, words that stir up the senses work better than abstract concepts. Notice how Jesus uses Gehenna in Mark 9:42-48:

Mark 9:42: "And if anyone causes one of these little ones who believe in me to sin, it would be better for him to be thrown into the sea with a large millstone tied around his neck."

If you cause someone to spiritually stumble, it would be better for you if you took the proverbial long walk on a short pier.

Mark 9:43: "If your hand causes you to sin, cut it off. It is better for you to enter life maimed than with two hands to go into hell [Gehenna], where the fire never goes out"
Mark 9:45: "And if your foot causes you to sin, cut it off. It is better for you to enter life crippled than to have two feet and be thrown into hell [Gehenna]"
Mark 9:47-48: "And if your eye causes you to sin, pluck it out. It is better for you to enter the kingdom of God with one eye than to have two eyes and be thrown into hell [Gehenna], where 'their worm does not die, and the fire is not quenched.'"

If a part of your body causes you to spiritually stumble, amputate.

Jesus says that if you convince someone not to believe in him (and the life of freedom from legalism that he brings), you would be better off thrown overboard in cement shoes. Jesus says you would be better off maimed but alive in his kingdom than whole and dead in the dump (where the worms never die and the fires never go out).

Jesus could have said, "Don't oppose my teaching." That idea expresses his meaning, but how dry and unmemorable! In the emotionally-charged language of Mark 9, is Jesus threatening people who fail to "get with the program" with a literal place of eternal, afterlife punishment? Let's answer that question with a few questions.

How literal was Jesus about drowning someone by putting a millstone around his neck and throwing him into the sea? How literal was he about amputating your hand? How literal was he about amputating your foot? How literal was he about plucking out your eyeball? Obviously none of these images are to be taken literally. He is speaking *figuratively* about millstone drownings, hand and foot amputations, eyeball pluckings and Hinnom Valley burnings.

So if nothing else in this parabolic saying is literal, then on what authority and for what reason can religion and its leaders dogmatically assume that Gehenna (the Hinnom Valley) is an illustration of a literal place of eternal torture?

Though much of Christendom has done so, I must tell you that religion's attempt to make Jesus' statements here into a hellfire and brimstone sermon fall far short of the gospel of Jesus Christ. Jesus is actually saying that when authoritarian, legalistic religious professionals scare the hell out of people they are, in fact, inviting those people to join them in their spiritual kingdom of hell.

The original audience who heard Jesus' words knew that living in Gehenna meant becoming garbage, sewage and filth. There was so much corruption and rot in that valley that generations of worms and maggots seemed to live forever, as they feasted on the garbage.

Legalistic religion today is in the same condition! Legalistic religion is a parasite which seems to go on and on and on, like the Energizer bunny you may have seen in television commercials advertising batteries.

Legalistic religion is a spiritual parasite that lives on the decaying bodies of the human hosts it enslaves, afflicting them with the idea that humans must gain God's favor based on their performance. Religion is death—Jesus is life! Performance-based religion is a kingdom of hell. God's grace is the kingdom of heaven.

The original audience who listened to Jesus knew the history of Gehenna as a valley of child sacrifice, a valley called *Topheth* (a place of fire), a burning dump and sewer. For Jesus' contemporary audiences, Gehenna was the perfect picture of a wasted life and a hellish existence. Who can live in Gehenna?

The obvious answer to this rhetorical question is no one. The original audience of Jesus knew that life was not possible in Jerusalem's trash-burning ditch. But a hellish spiritual existence is, poetically speaking, possible in the Gehenna of legalistic religion, as the teachers of the law and Pharisees demonstrated. Gehenna is Jesus' perfect metaphor for spiritual death.

Let's stop imposing a literal afterlife place of punishment on Jesus' teaching and look at what he is really saying. Jesus does not condemn anyone to eternal torture with his powerful illustration of spiritual death—rather, he paints a picture of life apart from God. Jesus' teaching is his invitation to life and freedom, an invitation to all, including the teachers of the law, the Pharisees and you and me.

Any recovering alcoholic will tell you that recovery begins with admitting you have a real, terminal problem with no free and easy way out. You do not ever stop being an alcoholic; you are alcoholic for life.

If your hand has to be holding a drink, then your hand

has dragged you with it into Gehenna. If your foot has to go to your local bar, then it has dragged the rest of you with it into Gehenna. If your eye can't stop looking at the alcohol you crave, then your eye will drag your entire body into Gehenna. If you are a recovering religious legalist, then the same warnings apply. Stay away from Christ-less religion—be an irreligious Christian!

It is better to cut yourself off from a habitual addiction, particularly when you have suffered from it in the past, than to keep intact your current actions and relationships which may only enable the addiction and thus eventually rob your life of freedom and spiritual rest in the kingdom of heaven. Jesus is saying that amputees can survive spiritually; but even those who are physically whole have no spiritual hope or future in an idolatrous burning dump.

My concern with the notion of the hell of eternal torment is the dogmatic insistence upon its reality by its advocates. Many claim that belief in a literal hell similar to Dante's mythical inferno is fundamental to Christianity! But, in his book, *Her Gates Will Never Be Shut*, Brad Jersak observes that many of the early church fathers maintained the *possibility* (not the presumption) of some version of judgment and hell and the twin *possibility* (not the presumption) that at the end of the day, no one need suffer it (page 8).

The teachers of the law and the Pharisees were addicted to religious performance. Religious performance had become their god. Religious performance had dragged them into Gehenna. But Jesus was not condemning them to hell. They were already there. He was prescribing religious amputation. It is either amputation of the burdens of religion or the suffering of hell it produces.

Evangelism—Saving People from Hell or Sending Them to Hell?

Matthew 23:15: "You travel over land and sea to win a single convert, and when he becomes one, you make him twice as much a son of hell as you are."

REJECTING RELIGION—EMBRACING GRACE

Within Christendom many churches use their members as virtual advertising agents, pressuring them into actively helping to "grow" the church. Not only do they burden their members with obligations concerning attendance, giving and volunteering, they also expect their members to recruit.

This practice is called "witnessing" and "evangelizing" within what are appropriately called "evangelical" churches. This recruiting effort plays a central role in a religious con which, according to Jesus, can make others twice as much a son of hell as those who recruit them.

How does "evangelism" within a religious culture work? Well, it works somewhat like a multi-level marketing program. Church members are encouraged to "reach out" to the *un-churched* or *unsaved* or *unbelievers* (interesting terms). Evangelism classes are held to teach members how to recruit new, unsuspecting members.

Of course, just like in multi-level marketing programs, church members are encouraged to "fish" for new members within the pool of healthy relationships they enjoy with friends and family—people who know and trust them. You've heard the line, "Trust me, I'm from the government and I'm here to help you." Well, you might also be wary of the line, "Trust me, I'm a member of the church down the street and I'm here to help you."

The most common method of religious persuasion is to work on the guilty conscience of the potential new recruit. One of the techniques is drawing a simple chart, depicting a deep chasm, with sinners on one side and a holy God on the other. The chasm depicts human separation from God created by sin. And then, once the church member illustrates the dilemma faced by the non-member, they illustrate the answer! The church member is trained to draw Jesus' cross as a bridge from one side to the other.

The new recruit is told all they need to do is walk across. So far, apart from changing some of the terminology and emphasis often used, and apart from changing some of the motivation behind the sales pitch, I would agree with the basic accuracy of the depiction. But, the pitch does not end there.

If a new recruit wants to "walk across" the chasm, that means, generally, walking down the aisle of a building that identifies itself as a church, shaking the preacher's hand, praying what is called a "sinner's prayer" and making a "public profession" of faith—that is, the potential recruit is told, accepting Jesus as their personal Lord and Savior. Within many spiritual addresses in Christendom this process of recruiting new members is called "building the church" or "growing the church" on the part of those doing the recruiting. On the part of the person joining the group, the carrot that is offered is called *salvation*.

Now comes the appeal to fear. What happens if the unchurched/unsaved/unbeliever non-member doesn't "get saved" and "evangelized?" If you "get saved" you won't spend eternity in hell. If you fail to "get saved?" I hope you like pain. Within the evangelical community this pitch is often called "selling fire insurance."

Putting aside this non-biblical definition of salvation for a moment, let's consider the ulterior motive. "Evangelism" and "witnessing" are not just about "saving" people from the presumed eternity of torture in hell the "lost" will endure. It is also about increasing the religious organization's membership and revenue (the new recruit will not only fill a chair or a pew, when they become a fully fledged convert they will contribute to the coffers).

It's the **ABCs** of organized religion: **A**ttendance, **B**uildings and **C**ash. The longstanding method of "church growth" favored by the majority of evangelical churches, though variously explained and practiced, is summarized by the following:

1. Convince the recruit of the grave danger of the eternal torment he/she faces because of his/her sins.
2. Convince him/her that God has provided a bridge to spiritual safety with Jesus' cross.

3. Convince him/her to walk across that bridge by attending your church and giving their life to religion (oops, I'm sorry, they actually say "to Christ").

4. Convert the person and add them to the list of members and contributors.

Is this a con? Yes. Church members are being encouraged to lure their family and friends into a recruitment ceremony. Church members are persuaded that they need to convince family and friends to attend this ceremony because they are in danger of eternal torture in hell. Then, once they are in the confines of the church, the pastor will attempt to "close the deal" and pressure those who are in attendance into membership and financial contributions. Is this a burden? Yes. For their part, church members feel that they are genuinely helping loved ones and friends—because they have been taught their efforts can actually save their loved ones and friends from an eternity of torture.

But the religious recruiters are convincing their "victims" of something that is only partially true. It is not entirely true that sin separates us from God. God does not run from sin. In Jesus Christ, according to Scripture, Jesus ran *to* sin. He embraced sinners with true friendship, accepting them and loving them. The Apostle Paul even says that Jesus *became* sin. And the Apostle John says that he *took away* the sin of the world. Paul further says that nothing, "neither death nor life, neither angels nor demons, neither the present nor the future, nor any powers, neither height nor depth, nor anything else in all creation, will be able to separate us from the love of God that is in Christ Jesus our Lord" (Romans 8:38-39). The whole point of God coming in sinful flesh was that sin could no longer separate us from a loving God.

Is there a perceived separation? Yes, from our end. Do we subjectively feel separation? Yes, from our end. But in Jesus our perception of separation is rejected. God has said a final and definitive "No" to sin and separation. All is forgiven. The only question is whether we trust and rest in this objective truth of Scripture. We were forgiven and reconciled to God before we ever asked. While we were yet sinners, Christ died for us. You can trust this objective claim, or you can trust your own subjective perception. You can trust Jesus, or you can trust religion.

Can you imagine Jesus instructing his disciples to "evangelize" in some version of a multi-level marketing scheme, so that the kingdom of heaven could grow? "Peter, James, John and all you guys, listen up. Start with your friends and family and then go into all the world and tell everyone God has abandoned them. Tell them God is really unhappy unless and until they get with the program. Tell them God plans to torture them forever when they die unless they do something about it. Tell them they have to pledge allegiance to me in a ceremony where they join a religious institution, promise regular attendance and pledge at least a tenth of their income—and make sure to tell them that is "a tenth of their *gross* income, not net. Amen."

Jesus said he is the way, the truth and the life. How can you "bring" people to Jesus with manipulation, subtle sales gimmicks, pressure, half truths and ulterior motives? Evangelism, as it is practiced by many churches today, is a burden.

Getting people to join and give is not enough, however. The religious con goes on. To keep your salvation (a slippery state to maintain, they say) once you are on the inside looking out you must attend church weekly, read your Bible daily, pray daily and give money "faithfully." These are the basics, the bare minimum, which you must do in order to maintain your salvation.

But salvation maintenance is precarious. When you slip up, it is counted against you. In order to make sure they remain"saved," new converts are instructed they not only need to do-and-do-and-do all the rules and requirements, but they need to serve-and-serve-and-serve the church. The truly "saved" become deacons, members of committees, youth retreat leaders, sing in the choir and (if the new convert *really* wants to secure their salvation) they jump through all the necessary hoops to get ordained!

What made Jesus furious was the attempt to turn religious practices into a means of salvation. He blasted the religious leaders of his day for heaping heavy burdens on people—addicting and enslaving them to pills, potions and prescriptions administered by religious priests. For Jesus, it was more than a con—it was and is abuse.

The whole thing had become, in Jesus' day, a self-serving racket. "Stop making my Father's house into a marketplace," he commanded (John 2:16). Salvation is not for sale. You cannot buy it with money or service or credentials. And when you presume to sell what God alone imparts without price, woe unto you! When you intimidate people to keep running perpetually on a spiritual hamster wheel to maintain their salvation, woe unto you!

There are churches that do not employ such methods of evangelism. Some even abhor it. But, many of those churches are shrinking numerically and financially. Many churches which utilize modern evangelicalism's primary method of recruitment are "growing"—that is, gaining members, building bigger buildings and getting more money.

Is it possible that some have sold their souls to the **ABCs**: **A**ttendance, **B**uildings and **C**ash?

Religious leaders can easily fall into the trap of seeing their church and its "success" as a point of personal pride in the community and the world. Religious professionals find diminishing membership and income make them look inadequate and, beyond that, like a failure, to their peers and acquaintances. It becomes a matter of saving face. It can all easily become a game, including acting and *appearances*. Jesus calls it *hypocrisy*.

Evangelism to "a" Church or "the" Church?

Church is far more than a building we frequent, a place we "go"—rather it is something we, by God's grace, "are." We can, if we so choose, become a member of "a" church but God alone places us in "the" church. We can be a part of "the" church, by God's grace, and not be involved in "a" church and all of its activities.

If we do find ourselves in "a" church (and if we choose to continue that relationship) we must remember some of the potential difficulties. We must remember that our relationship with "the" universal body of Christ, over which he presides as head, is the basis of our relationship with God. We must always remember that earthly religious organizations do not define our relationship with God. They may detract from our relationship with God, they may enhance it, or our membership in "a" church can have virtually nothing to do with our relationship with God.

When humans organize and buy land and build a building for religious purposes, something inevitably happens. The organization, intended initially to care for one another and serve in the community and world, demands maintenance. You have to pay for buildings and staff, and you want attractive buildings and a good staff.

Membership and attendance, rather than a means to ministry, becomes the end. Then rather than the institution being a tool with which to serve the world, the people turn inward and become tools to serve the institution. The result can be, and often is, ugly.

Remember that the gospel is good news to everyone. It is collective. The gospel calls us to love one another and serve the world. By contrast, religious institutions can degenerate into selfish, cliquish clubs.

What do you do when suddenly the cart is before the horse, when people put the **ABCs** (**A**ttendance, **B**uildings and **C**ash) before the gospel? "A" church which is founded as a part of the kingdom of heaven can morph into the kingdom of religion. Can the negative evolution be reversed?

Can part of "the" church be "a" church in such a way that the doctrines, creeds, regulations, institutionalism, organization and hierarchy do not become an idol that enslaves us?

All churches are, like individual Christians, works in progress. There are healthy churches which are grace-based and Christ-centered. There are churches which seem to be hopelessly enslaved to religious legalism, tradition and authoritarianism. Some churches are weak. Some churches are more than weak—they are toxic and deserve to die. But nothing is impossible with God. God can do whatever he wishes to whenever he wants—I know that, for I was trapped in a cultic swamp, with no way out.

Jesus is the fundamental, absolutely necessary ingredient in our relationship with God. At some point, when God offers us his grace, through Jesus, if we are to be in Christ, we must acknowledge our spiritual blindness. We must accept our need. I believe the act of acknowledging our spiritual blindness and seeking the healing of the Great Physician involves losing our religion.

There is no way forward, in Christ, for you or for me without the humble admission that we do not know the way forward. But that is our hope! It is profoundly paradoxical. The admission of spiritual blindness is the beginning of sight. The admission of death is the beginning of resurrection. Anything is possible with God.

The modern evangelism many experience today begins with the threat of eternal torture in hell. That is God's default setting for all of us, they say. That does not sound like good news to me. Yet this claim is the foundation not only for bad news evangelism today, but also for religious self-salvation programs offered in sermon after sermon, church after church, Sunday after Sunday.

When authentic Christianity is reduced to a behavior-modification program, God's grace is lost in "translation." When the focus of preaching and teaching is sin management, the gospel is no longer good news.

Self-salvation programs are action steps you can take, according to religion, to pull yourselves out, by your own bootstraps, of the hell they say that God is going to throw you into, if you fail to "get with the program." This is a fear-driven religious addiction that amounts to a life of hell—a life of Gehenna.

In much of modern evangelism, only lip service is given to Jesus' salvation of the world, the salvation that saves the world from Christ-less religion! According to legalistic religion, salvation does not go into effect until you perform prescribed religious steps. Such steps involve, at the very least, a sincere sinner's prayer, church membership, weekly worship attendance, tithing, daily prayer and daily Bible reading. None of these are bad things in and of themselves. Yet they are presented as the means whereby you get and stay saved.

Unlike in the Bible, where faith is trusting and resting in the message of salvation presented in Scripture, the modern evangelism proclaimed within Christendom is too often presented as a behavior-modification program enabling you to get and keep salvation for yourself.

But Christ-centered faith is not a religious program. Christ-centered faith is not focused on sin management! Accepting God's grace is taking the risk of trusting the truth of an unprovable assertion that your salvation is the gracious gift of God won for you and everyone else on the cross of Jesus.

Doubt is defined by many as the opposite of faith. That's not true. The opposite of faith is not doubt. It is fear. Doubts are absolutely necessary to faith because doubts—honest questions—demonstrate a depth of concern and express urgency for seeking the truth for your life. Doubts say that you really care enough to ask honest questions.

The message and motive of modern evangelism begins with fear of eternal torture in hell. If fear is the opposite of faith, then isn't it an act of un-grace to use fear to convince someone they need to come to faith? Fear cannot lead to authentic faith. Fear and faith are mutually exclusive. How can we manipulate people with fear and call it faith?

1 John 4:18-19: "There is no fear in love. But perfect love drives out fear, because fear has to do with punishment. The one who fears is not made perfect in love. We love because he first loved us.

Fear is a faithless, loveless emotion. Basing everything on fear of punishment denies the love of God, for motivating others by fear is not of God.

1 John 4:12: "…if we love one another, God lives in us and his love is made complete in us."

The religious, legal program of the teachers of the law and Pharisees was based on fear. They traveled far and wide to make a convert and promptly welcomed that unfortunate soul into their own hell on earth (Matthew 23:15).

The religious professionals of Jesus' day believed, as so many religious addicts do today, that the only way to please God and earn a blessed afterlife was to do everything prescribed in the law. Christ-less religion believes that how God feels about you at the end of your life depends entirely upon your performance. Fear of not performing well is based on the fear of God being displeased with your performance and the resulting punishment.

Religion is always based on fear of something. We are naturally afraid of hell, so religion offers us a program, but the program keeps us in fear that we will not perform well enough to avoid hell! Christ-less religion offers fear to fix fear.

Christless religion offers to "save" us from eternal torment by luring us into its own hell. It's a damnable hamster wheel heading for Gehenna! The teachers of the law and Pharisees were children of hell, Jesus said. They were fear-based, religious actors. And they were sending out fear-mongering missionaries to convert more fear-imprisoned children of hell.

Our Prayer:

Lord, our lives are being stolen by our fear-based ceremonies, customs, addictions and obsessions. We are addicted to religious performance. We have failed to trust and rest in your salvation as a gift. We are all recovering religionists, and we crave your love which will cast out all our fear. Let our honest doubts lead to faith in you and your unconditional love. And cause the love you give us to be shared with others, drawing them to lives of freedom and faith in you.

Chapter 5

Blind Leading the Blind

"Woe to you, blind guides! You say, 'If anyone swears by the temple, it means nothing; but if anyone swears by the gold of the temple, he is bound by his oath.' You blind fools! Which is greater: the gold, or the temple that makes the gold sacred? You also say, 'If anyone swears by the altar, it means nothing; but if anyone swears by the gift on it, he is bound by his oath.' You blind men! Which is greater: the gift, or the altar that makes the gift sacred? Therefore, he who swears by the altar swears by it and by everything on it. And he who swears by the temple swears by it and by the one who dwells in it. And he who swears by heaven swears by God's throne and by the one who sits on it."—Matthew 23:16-22

In the third woe of Matthew 23 Jesus calls the powerful, dangerous and well-educated religious authorities "blind guides," "blind fools" and "blind men." Jesus specifically takes them, or rather their religious beliefs, to task for their blind teachings concerning swearing.

In this chapter we will see that the pretentious posturing of religion, and its obsession with trivialities, leads to idolatry. We will see that Christ-less religion is blind!

Jesus seems to have gone out of his way to heal blind

people. Matthew and Luke record the healing of many blind men in Galilee (Matthew 9:27-31, 12:22, 15:30-31, Luke 7:21), and Mark relates the story of the healing of a blind man at Bethsaida in detail (Mark 8:22-26). Jesus healed the blind in Jericho (Matthew 20:30-34; Mark 10:46-52; Luke 18:35-43), and in the temple in Jerusalem (Matthew 21:14). An entire chapter of John's gospel tells the story of a blind man whom Jesus healed and sent to the pool of Siloam to wash (John 9). Why was healing the blind so important to Jesus?

The blind were barred by the priests from entering the temple precincts in Jerusalem because Jewish religious practices deemed them to be "impure." That is why Jesus talked about inviting the poor, the crippled, the blind and the lame to banquets, symbolizing the spiritual banquet in which God includes those whom the temple authorities had banned (Luke 14:12-24).

Jesus was breaking down barriers erected by religious professionals. He was establishing the inclusion of all God's children and he was making a clear, unambiguous statement opposing any impediment, physical or spiritual, to the worship of God.

Another reason why Jesus healed the blind is illustrated in John 9. Jesus uses his own spit to make mud. In movies, this healing scene shows Jesus smearing mud on the blind man's *eyelids*. But such depictions may be diminishing what John is describing.

John might be telling us that Jesus put mud balls in the man's empty eye sockets. It may well have been that Jesus, the second person of the Godhead, the Creator (Colossians 1:16) formed new eyeballs from mud for this blind man. This creative act harkens back to Genesis 2:4-7 where the Creator forms the first man from mud (Adam's name means earth creature, or *mud man*, if you will).

Through this healing Jesus proclaims that he is the God-man, God in the flesh and that he is Creator (John 1:1-3, 10; Hebrews 1:1-2). After all, if the Creator can make a whole man from mud, how hard is it for the God-man to create new eyeballs for a mud-man?

Jesus healing the blind is a symbol pointing to his mission to heal spiritual blindness. In his sermon at Nazareth he read from a scroll of the book of Isaiah:

Luke 4:18-19: "The Spirit of the Lord is on me, because he has anointed me to preach good news to the poor. He has sent me to proclaim freedom for the prisoners and recovery of sight for the blind, to release the oppressed, to proclaim the year of the Lord's favor."

Then Jesus announced that he was the fulfillment of Isaiah's prophesy (Isaiah 61:1-2):

Luke 4:20-21: "Then he rolled up the scroll, gave it back to the attendant and sat down. The eyes of everyone in the synagogue were fastened on him, and he began by saying to them, 'Today this scripture is fulfilled in your hearing.'"

Jesus came to liberate people from spiritual control and oppression. And he came to pronounce that now is the time of God's favor —God's unmerited and undeserved grace. So when Jesus literally cured a blind person, it was a sign of his mission to cure spiritual blindness. Nowhere in Scripture is this clearer than in John 9.

In John 9, a man cured of blindness by Jesus is interrogated by the Judean authorities. They couldn't see that Jesus, a man whom they considered to be a Sabbath breaker, could be from God. Not satisfied with the healed man's testimony, they interrogated his parents. Still the authorities were not satisfied. They released the man, but apparently had him followed. Jesus found the man and explained the goals and objectives of his ministry.

John 9:39: "Jesus said, 'For judgment I have come into this world, so that the blind will see and those who see will become blind.'"

Jesus' healing of this man obviously has greater significance than merely an individual act of healing for a single man. It is a highly symbolic act pointing as a sign to his larger mission involving spiritual blindness.

The word "judgment" in this passage does not mean condemnation. The biblical Greek word is *krisis*, from which we get our English word "crisis." The Greek word means literally *under division.* The presence of Jesus and his words are a crisis because of the effects they have on people. He and his words divide friends and family. As a result of his presence and his message, those who know they are spiritually blind begin to see. And those who think they can see are confronted with their blindness.

John 9:40: "Some Pharisees who were with him heard him say this and asked, 'What? Are we blind too?'"

The Pharisees perceived *krisis* in Jesus' statement. And they were right. Jesus clearly means more than the lack of physical vision when he uses the word "blind." He means blindness to truth. Truth is, of course, personified through his presence and preaching (John 14:6). Jesus came to expose the blindness of those who thought they had spiritual insight and perception, to give spiritual vision to those who were aware of their spiritual blindness, and to heal the blindness of those who were willing to face their need of spiritual vision. Jesus responds to the Pharisees:

John 9:41: "Jesus said, 'If you were blind, you would not be guilty of sin; but now that you claim you can see, your guilt remains.'"

By presuming spiritual insight, the Pharisees were clinging to their guilt. How can you experience forgiveness unless you see and acknowledge your sin? God doesn't force anyone to accept his free gift of forgiveness, and it seems the Pharisees exercised their choice to reject his forgiveness.

In their presumption of innocence, the Pharisees said that they didn't need Jesus to help them with their spiritual vision, an audacious statement which was evidence of their continuing, defiant blindness. The Pharisees, of course, were not just blind to their own sin. They were also blind to who Jesus was. In the first chapter of the Gospel of John we read:

John 1:9-11: "The true light that gives light to every man was coming into the world. He was in the world, and though the world was made through him, the world did not recognize him. He came to that which was his own, but his own did not receive him."

Jesus was the one true light, but unless they were healed the spiritually blind could not see his true identity. The blind cannot see the light. In the case of the confrontation in John 9 the Pharisees refused to accept the offer of spiritual healing. They not only failed to recognize him, they also failed to receive him. They were so accustomed to spiritual darkness the Light of the world (John 9:5) hurt their eyes.

Can You See?

As our lives progress, we all have experiences that we have never had before. Early in life many of these never-before experiences are exciting, but as we age, some of the "new" experiences are ones we would rather do without, but they arrive nonetheless.

Eight years ago my wife Karen and I had a new experience which involved the feared word "cancer." Without invitation, warning or announcement, like a venomous snake, cancer attacked. We had one of those new experiences we had never had before. In 2002 Karen had surgery for that cancer, in her neck and her tonsils, and over the years of her recovery we came to believe that she was cancer free. We believed that particular kind of cancer in that particular part of her body would probably never come back.

It did. Just before Easter, 2010, Karen started to feel lumps in the lymph nodes of the side of her neck that was not operated on in the first surgery. We once again found ourselves on an emotional roller coaster ride of tests and consultations to help us determine what course of action we should take.

In early May, 2010, Karen had surgery for the same kind of cancer, on the other side of her neck. It was the same kind of cancer she had eight years earlier, and the operation took place in the same hospital with the same surgeon. We thank God for the peace, comfort and healing he graciously gave her and our family during the surgery and the nearly seven weeks of radiation treatments that followed.

During this second close encounter with cancer our conversations became incredibly focused. We found that we were "looking at" people differently. God's grace has a way of making us far more aware and sensitized to the suffering and pain experienced by others—not only the specific trials and specific people about whom we are aware and for whom we pray—but for all those unknown traumas that people endure every day in this sick and dying world.

There are times when we stop at a stoplight and as we glance to our right or left, we find ourselves not simply seeing just another driver, but someone who might be going through a painful divorce. We realize that some of the people we pass as we wheel our shopping cart through the grocery store are dealing with family, financial and health issues. When we sit near others at Starbucks or wait in line with them at a pharmacy, we appreciate that some of those people may well have just heard devastating news in a doctor's office.

The recent blockbuster movie, *Avatar*, introduced a new phrase to our vocabularies. *I see you*, used within the context of the movie, communicated an emotional connection, a spiritual perception that transcends external details of gender, race, age and class. *I see you* has come to mean, for me at least, an acknowledgement of the broken and fragmented life of another fellow human being (I am aware of the emotionally supercharged discussions about the degree to which the ideas advanced by *Avatar* are pagan, but that's another discussion). When we live in Christ and he lives in us *I see you* can speak of the spiritual dimension, in which, by God's grace, we are enabled to see through the eyes of Jesus.

A man named Simon once hosted Jesus at a dinner, and during the dinner a woman of questionable character crashed the party to see Jesus. At best Simon saw the woman as an uninvited guest, someone whose social status did not entitle her to be a guest at his home. Beyond that, Simon probably viewed her with disdain—she was a street person, the scum of the earth.

Jesus asked Simon, "Do you see this woman?" (Luke 7:44). The woman was all but invisible to Simon and the other polite, church-going, religious people at the dinner. What did Jesus see when he saw the woman?

Matthew 9:36: "When he saw the crowds, he had compassion on them, because they were harassed and helpless, like sheep without a shepherd."

During his earthly life Jesus saw the real struggles, the real heartaches, the internal battles faced by those to whom he ministered. He identified with them—he still identifies with all of us. He came here, as God in the flesh, to know us, to have compassion on us and empathy for us. He came to see us.

Jesus not only sees us, but when he heals us of our spiritual blindness, he enables us to see with his eyes. I am convinced that he can use our suffering to enhance our spiritual vision. We see with the eyes of Jesus when we follow in his footsteps, as Peter says:

1 Peter 2:21: "To this were you called, because Christ suffered for you, leaving you an example, that you should follow in his steps."

This passage is often explained as an exhortation to orchestrate our religious behavior so that we carefully duplicate Jesus' actions. However, the passage does not suggest that meaning. When people believe such a twisted and distorted interpretation of this passage, Christ-less religion is having its way with them. The passage says that we are called to suffer, just as Jesus did.

There is no doubt that North American Christians have an inadequate view of what Christ-centered suffering is all about—and much of the blame lies at the door of religious institutions who take the easy way out. It's far more popular to tell folks that God wants them to be rich and healthy than it is to proclaim the gospel that our journey in Christ will often take us through the valley of the shadow of death. But it is in suffering that God causes us to:

2 Peter 3:18: "...grow in the grace and knowledge of our Lord and Savior Jesus Christ."

Years ago I gave a sermon on suffering. I think I was about 30 years old. At the time I was studying the principles of the art and practice of homiletics (preaching). I had just learned an axiom which preachers are often taught—"there's a broken heart in every pew." Suffering is always a relevant, necessary and critically important part of our lives. Everyone suffers during their lives, and everyone desires to find meaning in their suffering. Understood properly from a Christ-centered perspective, suffering always leads us back to Christ and his cross. Paul said:

1 Corinthians 2:2: "For I resolved to know nothing while I was with you except Jesus Christ and him crucified."

As I prepared for that sermon, I read a story about a young pastor who had given a sermon about suffering and was talking, after church, with an older gentleman. The older gentleman was—well he was about my age now. The older man was thanking the pastor for the sermon, and then he said, "Pastor, I have one suggestion. Would you give that sermon again in about 30 years?"

More than three decades have passed since that particular sermon I gave on suffering, and thank God, he has transformed me in many ways. By God's grace I'm able to speak to the issue of suffering with spiritual vision and Christ-centeredness I did not have as a young man.

While there's no doubt that much of what I have experienced and endured over the past 30 years has been through self-inflicted suffering, more recently I have, by God's grace, glimpsed another kind of growth "in the grace and knowledge of our Lord and Savior Jesus Christ."

I believe that God helps to ease you and me through some painful realities which we don't necessarily cause or deserve, but realities that we nevertheless experience. Suffering is not only the stuff of life itself, apart from God—but suffering, following in the footsteps of Jesus, is at the very foundation of our relationship with God.

Allow me to share with you a letter I received just a few days before my wife's second cancer surgery. It was one of those experiences that I believe God used to sharpen my spiritual vision—a communication that further sensitized me so that I may see others through the eyes of Jesus.

Dear Greg,

My wife Carol and I became a part of your online congregation years ago. Every Sunday we joined you and others, online, at Christianity Without the Religion (CWR). We read all your books—PTM and CWR were our church, and you still are for me.

But three weeks ago, with our family by her side, my wife passed away peacefully at home. She battled 16 years with that dreaded cancer.

*We were married for almost 45 years. We found an excellent pastor who spoke at the funeral, remarking about my wife's faith in Jesus and about CWR—our church. As he prepared for the funeral the pastor picked up your book which my wife was reading before she became too sick to continue—*Spiritual Soup for the Hungry Soul. *He talked about that book as one she was reading before her death.*

She died one day before my birthday—a lousy birthday present. We used to "attend" Sunday services at CWR together—now I will be attending alone. I miss her terribly. All alone and lonely.

— Nova Scotia, Canada

Give thanks for the spiritual vision God grants you, for truly we have no spiritual vision unless our eyes are opened and we see Jesus. Ask Jesus to help you see others through his eyes, the eyes of grace. By God's grace, we become more aware of the profound suffering of all God's children.

Spiritual Blindness and Swearing

In the **third woe** of Matthew 23 (signature verses for this chapter) Jesus calls the teachers of the law and Pharisees "blind." John 9 helps us see the totality of what it means when one is blinded by religion. These religious professionals in John 9 were blind to their own sin. They were completely in the dark about Jesus and his healing ministry.

They were so blind to the suffering and needs of others that when Jesus healed the blind man they could only react with condemnation and criticism. They weren't happy the blind man had been healed—they were upset because their religious authority was questioned. Here in Matthew 23 Jesus explained that they were also blind with regard to their own erroneous teachings about swearing.

In this third woe of Matthew 23 Jesus is exposing religious rituals of swearing to be irrelevant and irreverent. Jesus' teaching is that swearing about anything is a pathetic practice because it is a testimony to human dishonesty. If we were honest, then why would we need to swear oaths?

Some take what Jesus says about swearing literally, and refuse to be sworn in by a court of law, and instead will say "I affirm." The difference between saying "I swear" and "I affirm" is a matter of semantics. Jesus is not teaching us that the word "swear" is a profane word. Jesus is not suggesting that swearing in a civil or legal setting is a sin. What Jesus is teaching goes to the core reason why humans believe they need to swear—because dishonesty is rife! Jesus is saying that there is no need to support our statements with oaths and formulas that underscore our sincerity.

We swear on our mother's grave, we swear on a stack of Bibles, and we swear to God. We cross our hearts and hope to die when swearing to tell the truth, and we cross our fingers when we lie. Before we testify in a court of law we place our hands on a Bible and swear to tell the truth, the whole truth, and nothing but the truth, "so help me God." When the United States president is "sworn in" he repeats the oath of office, by saying that very phrase: "So help me God."

For the sake of clarity, let me state the obvious. Swearing and cursing are not the same things. Cursing is using profanity. Swearing is pledging an oath of truth. The third commandment in the old covenant says not to take the Lord's name in vain, which means do not swear by God's name when, in fact, you are lying. The swearing to which Jesus has reference is concerned with perjury, not profanity.

Jesus' problem with the scribes and Pharisees concerning swearing has to do with their teachings concerning how to pledge an oath of truth in a religious setting or for religious reasons. Earlier in Matthew, in what is often called the "sermon on the mount" Jesus gave the same teaching, in a more general way:

Matthew 5:33-37: "Again, you have heard that it was said to the people long ago, 'Do not break your oath, but keep the oaths you have made to the Lord.' But I tell you, Do not swear at all: either by heaven, for it is God's throne; or by the earth, for it is his footstool; or by Jerusalem, for it is the city of the Great King. And do not swear by your head, for you cannot make even one hair white or black. Simply let your 'Yes' be 'Yes,' and your 'No,' 'No'; anything beyond this comes from the evil one."

Here in Matthew 23 Jesus builds on his earlier statement about swearing in the "sermon on the mount" to address the ludicrous lengths to which performance based religion takes us—specifically in attempting to assure others that we are telling the truth.

While exposing yet another way in which religion becomes a preposterous burden, Jesus bemoans the phony and disastrous leadership of religious professionals who themselves do not know God. He calls religious professionals spiritually blind—unmasking them—exposing them as incapable of helping others to know God—and in this third woe he does so three times!

Jesus reveals the stupidity of religious teaching that deemed an oath sworn by the temple to be inadequate, while regarding an oath sworn by the gold adorning the temple as acceptable. He strips the religious veneer off the idea that simply swearing by the altar is deficient and ineffective, while suggesting that a more elaborate oath based on a gift on the altar will "do the trick." Chicanery and deceit are exactly what Jesus is getting at. In this third woe he is turning the light on the flim-flam artists of religious dog-and-pony shows.

The only way to explain why otherwise reasonable people would fall for such far-fetched ideas is the fact that they are spiritually blind. They are spiritually blind because they believe that God can be pleased and placated by formulaic incantations. They are blind because they believe that furniture and buildings are holy, rather than God himself. Because they are spiritually blind, they are easily deceived and seduced into idolatry.

Jesus is saying that if the teachers believe that the gold makes the temple sacred, and they believe that the sacrificial offering makes the altar sacred, then, logically, they must also believe that the temple and the altar make God sacred! That, my friends, is backwards. That, my friends, is idolatry. Do you see it?

1. If the gold makes the temple sacred, then it follows logically that the temple makes God sacred.

2. If the sacrifice makes the altar sacred, then it follows logically that the altar makes God sacred.

Idolatry in Christendom Today

An obsession with spiritual trivialities can replace relationship with God with idolatry—relationship with religious rituals and ceremonies. When the word "idolatry" is read or mentioned today, most people think of primitive, superstitious practices of bowing down to statues and literal idols. But idolatry is far more pervasive than simple superstition. Idolatry has to do with anything we believe to have spiritual significance or relevance, other than God. Idolatry is the act of putting any practice or any individual or any desire before God.

Jesus insisted that we put the kingdom of heaven first (Matthew 6:33). He explained that excessive worry and attention to food and drink and clothes makes these things idols in our lives. He warned that money can do that too. And as we saw in our discussion of Gehenna, any number of behaviors or practices can become desperate addictions that separate us from real spiritual life and freedom in Christ. When that happens, the objects of our unhealthy attachments become idols, and those idols drag us into a spiritual hell.

The **ABCs** of organized religion—**A**ttendance, **B**uildings and **C**ash—have become the focus of fear-driven religious idolatry. The intensity of worry about these priorities within Christendom today cannot be understated. Churches are supposed to be people who together extend the ministry of Christ in the world.

But now we call buildings churches. Religious institutions have created complex organizations that require management of properties and buildings. And the properties and buildings demand maintenance. To maintain them, the focus slowly shifts away from reaching out, and the focus becomes more and more about internal, institutional maintenance.

To pay for buildings, you need cash. To get more cash, you need more members. Before you know it, membership and money become the means of serving the buildings. This all-important search for ways to increase membership and money dominates the conversation at many church meetings.

As we discussed in chapter four, in the name of evangelism, in the name of church growth, members of the church are enlisted as workers to somehow entice more people into their church. Their church thus becomes a voracious monster. In many places within Christendom church itself has become a god—a god named *Growth*. The *Growth*-god consumes its members' (slaves?) time, treasures and talents. The worship of the **ABCs** (**A**ttendance, **B**uildings and **C**ash) has turned some churches into idols.

Bibliolatry

The big business of religion has turned virtually every physical trapping used in ceremonies and rituals and services into some kind of idol. Some within Christendom have made the Bible itself into an idol! There truly is nothing new under the sun. The religion of Jesus' day and its authorities had turned the Old Testament scriptures into an idol. Jesus addressed this idolatry:

John 5:39-40: "You diligently study the Scriptures because you think that by them you possess eternal life. These are the Scriptures that testify about me, yet you refuse to come to me to have life."

The Scriptures (capitalized as a proper noun, not because they are deity!) are simply paper and ink. The Bible is not the fourth member of the Trinity. The Bible is, however, a collection of words written by people inspired by God, and those words point to Jesus, the one who has life, gives life and is life. In some religious traditions, when the term "Word of God" is used it means the Bible. However, the Bible itself calls Jesus "the Word of God."

John 1:1, 14, 17: "In the beginning was the Word, and the Word was with God, and the Word was God... The Word became flesh and made his dwelling among us. We have seen his glory, the glory of the One and Only, who came from the Father, full of grace and truth...For the law was given through Moses; grace and truth came through Jesus Christ."

Revelation 19:13: "He is dressed in a robe dipped in blood, and his name is the Word of God."

The Bible never refers to itself as "the Word of God." Blasphemy? Yes, the Bible records the "word of God" (lowercase "w") or the "word of the Lord" (lowercase "w") spoken by prophets, by Jesus, or by the apostles. And yes, those words are recorded in the Bible. But "the Word of God" (uppercase, truly *big* "W") is a title reserved for a deity, not paper and ink.

The phrase "Word of God" is reserved exclusively for Jesus. Jesus alone, says the Bible, is the Word of God. It is not the words that make the Word sacred, but the Word that makes the words sacred. The furniture, hardware, ceremonies and trappings of religion are often elevated to pre-eminent positions, so that they, rather than God, occupy the spotlight. In such an environment even the Bible can become an idol.

Clergiolatry

Because humans are easily persuaded, many tend to practically worship religious leaders. Religious professionals are often put on a pedestal, sometimes with their cooperation, sometimes in spite of their protests.

Within the world of religion, there are many subtle and not-so-subtle ways to encourage the semi-deification of religious professionals—after all, if religious authorities are "blessed," "anointed," "prophetic" and/or "apostolic," then the real winner is religion. Such practices keep the pews filled. Paul had something to say about this practice. Yes, even way back then people boasted about who had the "holiest" pastor:

1 Corinthians 1:11-15: "My brothers, some from Chloe's household have informed me that there are quarrels among you. What I mean is this: One of you says, 'I follow Paul'; another, 'I follow Apollos'; another, 'I follow Cephas'; still another, 'I follow Christ.' Is Christ divided? Was Paul crucified for you? Were you baptized into the name of Paul? I am thankful that I did not baptize any of you except Crispus and Gaius, so no one can say that you were baptized into my name."

To whatever degree that you look to a religious professional, remember that he or she has no special spiritual mojo with which to make it rain and ward off pestilence. If you attend a brick-and-mortar church, it's fine to ask your pastor to pray for you. But know this—God has not given out his personal cell phone number only to people who have graduated from a seminary. God hears your prayers as well. God hears a little child's prayers.

If you read Christian authors, if you listen to and allow a Christian ministry to serve you, realize that they and their leadership are simply humans—just like you. Idolizing religious professionals is spiritually unhealthy. God may use humans as his hands and feet to help you, but the real focus of your faith and worship is Jesus.

Don't allow religion and all of its wiles to lead you down the garden path. Don't be deceived—religious "holy" places are anything but holy. God alone is holy. God can use the Bible to reveal himself to you and me, but the Bible is not the Word of God. Jesus is the one and only Word of God.

God can use a physical building which calls itself "a" church to help you. But your real focus as a Christ follower is "the" church and the head of "the" church—Jesus. You may choose to attend "a" church, or you may choose not to. You may choose to allow a physical human being to, within his or her limitations, help you come to know God. But the true Pastor and Shepherd of our souls is Jesus.

Our Prayer:
Lord, open our blind eyes and expose the idolatry in our lives, the blind, unhealthy attachments we have to people and things. Remove the scales from our eyes so that we can clearly see religious customs and ceremonies that obscure our relationship with you. Cause our idolatries to fail us so that we might turn to you. For you alone are holy, you alone are sacred, not the furniture of faith, not the ecclesiastical leaders and not even the Bible which you have inspired and preserved for us. Truly you and you alone are the Shepherd of our souls.

Chapter 6

Waiter—There's a Camel in My Soup!

"Woe to you, teachers of the law and Pharisees, you hypocrites! You give a tenth of your spices—mint, dill and cumin. But you have neglected the more important matters of the law—justice, mercy and faithfulness. You should have practiced the latter, without neglecting the former. You blind guides! You strain out a gnat but swallow a camel."—Matthew 23:23-24

*T*he Jesus I Never Knew by Philip Yancey is high on my list of life-changing books—it helped to introduce me to the Jesus I had never known. Because I can relate to so many of the experiences Yancey shares, I often find myself going back to the well worn pages of my copy to revisit an example or illustration he provides. One I particularly relate to is when Yancey talks of his tenure as a student attending Moody Bible Institute, the conservative Bible college.

At the time Yancey attended Moody, the college had a rule banning all male students from wearing mustaches, beards and "long hair" (defined as below the ears). Even while they resented this oppressive rule, Yancey relates how he and other students walked past a large oil painting of Dwight L. Moody every day, on their way to class. The painting clearly illustrated that the illustrious founder of the college was not in compliance with the rules imposed on young male students at the time Yancey was enrolled.

Later in his life Yancey was leading a group discussion with survivors of Christian Bible colleges and fundamentalist churches. When the group started to swap "war stories" about hypocritical legalism Yancey told them the rules about hair length at Moody and what seemed to him and others to be the hypocrisy of the prominently displayed painting of the founder who was clearly in violation of those rules. Hypocrisy is particularly galling when authorities don't seem willing to play by the rules they impose on us, so that they, in effect say, "Do as I say, not as I do."

When he told this story, Yancey recounts that "Everyone laughed. Everyone except Greg, that is, who fidgeted in his seat and smoldered" (page 148). Greg finally came unglued, indignantly informing the group that they were accusing Moody Bible Institute of being Pharisees when they themselves were the real Pharisees—sitting in judgment, pretending that they were all "high and mighty and mature." When Greg finished, all eyes focused on Philip Yancey, waiting for his reply. But Yancey had no reply, because he recognized that Greg was correct—Yancey and the others were arrogant in their own self-righteousness, pointing out the hypocrisy in other's lives in such as way as to advance their own presumed moral supremacy.

As we have already noted, hypocrisy is acting—the act of wearing a mask, appearing to be someone other than the person behind the mask. Jesus spoke of spiritual rebirth as being somewhat like becoming a little child (Matthew 18:1-4). One thing that children cannot do well is wear a mask. They are who they are. They're not good poker players, because their faces tell adults exactly what they are thinking. Parents often say to their children, "I can read you like a book" (at least my mother assured me of that fact, and she was usually right).

Hypocrisy is so easy to see and identify in others, isn't

it? Mark Twain once said, "Nothing needs to be reformed as much as other people's habits." And when other people's habits are hypocritical, when they are two-faced, then we are often outraged. Hypocrisy is often called "not practicing what you preach."

The hypocrisy that Jesus condemns is rank hypocrisy — living in an arrogant, high-handed manner, expecting perfection of others while being virtually impervious to your own imperfections and flaws. Humility is, in many ways, the polar opposite of the attitude projected by blatant hypocrites, and humility is one of the chief attributes given to those in whom Jesus lives. Humility is the character trait that Jesus specifically offers as an illustration of those who have been changed, by God's grace, into little children (Matthew 18:4).

Humility keeps our hearts and minds on the big picture, whereas hypocrisy drives us to nitpick and condemn others, even about the smallest of issues. Hypocrisy makes life miserable for the hypocrite as well as those whom the hypocrite condemns. Author John Stott speaks of hypocrisy being, for Christians, what cancer is for the physical body. Hypocrisy demands perfection of ourselves and others, and thus poisons our relationship with God. Intense preoccupation with externals leads to a fascination with trivialities, which in turns drives us to hypocrisy, and when hypocrisy begins to have its way with us our desire to appear to be something we are not begins to choke any spiritual life that exists within our hearts and souls.

You may have heard the story of a "golf widow" who asked her husband why he wasn't golfing any more with his former golfing partner, Bob. As he headed out the door for the golf course, the husband responded to his wife, "Would you keep playing golf with a man who moved his golf ball a few feet closer to the hole when you weren't watching?" His wife was appalled, "Well, no, I wouldn't." Her husband said, "Well, neither will Bob."

The fourth woe of Matthew 23 is an unforgettable image! Once again Jesus calls the teachers of the law and the Pharisees hypocrites, this time because they filtered their water and wine just in case little hard-to-detect, unclean bugs (Leviticus 11:41-44) may have flown under their religious radar. This is surely one of Jesus' funniest one liners. While these religious leaders meticulously screened barely visible critters Jesus told them they gave little thought to swallowing a huge, humped quadruped. They couldn't see their King-Kong-sized spiritual problems because their spiritual microscopes were trained on preventing the intrusion of an "unclean" evil invader.

These religious "guides" spent their time and resources in a vain attempt to safeguard their world from little bugs —they were so engrossed with spiritual minutia that they overlooked the real enemy. Blind to the real spiritual threat, they swallowed the fruit of religion—the oppression and misery caused by all of its legalisms.

Jesus contrasted the leaders' meticulous tithing of home-grown spices and their simultaneous obliviousness to more important matters. They were majoring in the minors and minoring in the majors, and they seemed to be unaware that they were doing so. They believed they could make themselves righteous by their attention to detail. They were meticulous in details which did not amount to the proverbial hill of beans. Obsessing over trivialities is the camel in religion's cup, causing it to ignore/overlook/devalue the essentials.

Hypocritical Marketing of Sin

Within many religious environments and cultures, "strong" sermons about sin actually helps ensure that the synagogue/mosque/church is filled. Ranting and raving keeps the parking lot filled! Within Christendom specifically, there are at least two dynamics that contribute to the popularity of "strong" sermons:

1) Guilt and Self-Loathing. Christ-less religion has effectively convinced its followers that unless they feel somewhat like a worm, metaphorically capable of exiting the church following a sermon by crawling under its closed doors, then that sermon was not, by definition, a good ("strong") sermon. It's an expectation that many captives of legalistic religion have that borders on a sick, emotional dysfunction. Many church-goers feel so unloved by God they believe they deserve to be screamed and yelled at—the only way they can leave church feeling remotely good about themselves is if they have been spiritually abused. They believe God has every right to treat them like the spiritual road-kill that they are, so they actually feel better if they show up at church and bend over to take what they believe they have coming to them. Abusive religion has convinced them that the only way that their sins can be purged, and that they in turn can feel cleansed, is for them to take their licks. It's sick, but it's a strategic factor in keeping many churches filled.

2) Sin sells! Not only do some people keep coming back to church in a vain attempt to please God by letting his representatives shame and humiliate them, but they also return to hear rants about how bad other people are—especially those who are not in attendance. Religion provides a false spiritual oasis for its followers by denouncing, attacking and even ridiculing the sins of those who don't attend church—or at least that particular church. In this respect, the more fundamentalist churches can often feed and breed pride, arrogance, racism and bigotry, in their thinly-veiled diatribes against sin and sinners at large. When the harangues are specifically targeted at those who are unwelcome in such a religious culture, the captive audience feels better about themselves because such sins are not normally part of their lives. Tirades against gays, abortion and "liberal" politicians are examples of "strong sermons" that seem to convince the preacher and his congregation that the "stand" they take pleases God (which usually involves condemnation and sometimes derision—far from the compassion of Jesus). But while sermons about sins that are not believed to infect the congregation may provide a false comfort, ironically, problems which may be common to the congregation are seldom addressed, such as the toxic effects of habits like gluttony and smoking.

When it comes to the topic of sin, smug self-righteousness is not confined to those who believe that they are Christians. People who do not even pretend to be Christians often justify their lifestyles with statements like: "I'm a good person. I don't go around robbing and killing people. So I don't buy all this sin business spewed by Christians. Sin is just a word religious zealots use to condemn and control people. Church-goers are self-righteous hypocrites for pointing their fingers at everybody else. How can they believe that pew-warming makes them better persons than me?"

I do not disagree entirely with such statements. It is ironic that non-churchgoers can sometimes see the blindness inherent in any and all finger pointing more clearly than those who regularly frequent a building known as a church. Indeed, how can believers in Jesus (like you and me) forget that the Bible insists that *all* have sinned and fallen short (Romans 3:23), and *none* are righteous, *not even one* (Romans 3:10)? And how can those who have been forgiven much (Luke 7:47) fail to remember that finger pointing is judging others, as we are expressly told by Jesus (Matthew 7:1; Luke 6:37)?

Many church-goers identify sinners as those who don't attend church. In many fundamentalist churches and groups sinners are not simply those who fail to attend church—church-goers who don't attend "our" church are also branded as sinners. The logical conclusion is that church attendance itself, especially at the "right" church, can purge the sin out of a sinner.

Back in 1959 Johnny Horton had a hit song called "The Battle of New Orleans" which was quickly followed by a parody titled "The Battle of Kookamonga." Country singers Homer and Jethro wrote new lyrics, changing the context from a battleground to a campground, with combat replaced by Boy Scouts frantically trying to discover and spy on Girl Scouts. After detailing the boys' adventures chasing girls through the woods, by way of conclusion to their parody Homer and Jethro offered this sanctimonious justification —a moral to the story, which, at least in the minds of the Boy Scouts, absolved them from Girl Scout chasing and any related or unrelated sins: "A rooty toot toot, a rooty toot toot. Oh, we are the boys from the Boy Scout troop. We don't smoke, and we don't chew and we don't go with the girls that do."

You'll have to forgive my rather unsophisticated tastes when it comes to music, but those lyrics seem to capture the hilarious religious antics undertaken by many in an attempt to appear "holy" and sinless. Jesus offered the silly, hyperbolic picture of those who carefully ensured that their physical water and wine were free of miniscule bugs while thinking nothing of swallowing a spiritual camel. Many attempt to make their lives pure with physical behaviors, such as perfect church attendance and careful tithing while swallowing a spiritual camel—ignoring the real focus of God, including, as Jesus says, *justice, mercy and faithfulness.*

Just how important is that bumper sticker "Honk if you love Jesus" to God? Is God really keeping score of all the minivans that are adorned with a chrome "fish" as opposed to those that are not? Does God only answer the prayers of those who attend church—or perhaps just those who attend the "right" church?

Given their meticulous, exhaustive attempts to cleanse themselves from spiritual impurities the teachers of the law and Pharisees did not consider themselves to be corrupt and contaminated. They didn't think of themselves as sinners because they took great pains to filter out all of the bad stuff from their lives. Religion spends most of its time offering programs, activities and rituals which it claims will purify its followers on the one hand, and on the other identify and target sinners who are not "with the program" and who need to be "warned" (of eternal torture if they don't change their ways).

Sinners, by the definition given by the teachers of the law and Pharisees, were "outsiders" who did not keep all of the laws as prescribed and interpreted by them. The Apostle Paul spoke of his life as Saul, the Pharisee, who was "blameless" under the law (Philippians 3:4-6). Before God transformed him from the Saul of religion to the Paul of grace, Paul believed himself to have been diligent and successful in keeping every rule no matter how small. Yet, while believing this about himself, the Saul of religion mercilessly and relentlessly persecuted Christians. He was absolutely convinced his holy war against Christians was one and the same as the very work of God. The Saul of religion, a Pharisee who believed himself legally blameless before God, treated Christians with contempt, injustice and a complete lack of mercy. Such behavior is hardly what Micah had in mind.

Micah 6:6-8: "With what shall I come before the LORD and bow down before the exalted God? Shall I come before him with burnt offerings, with calves a year old? Will the LORD be pleased with thousands of rams, with ten thousand rivers of oil? Shall I offer my firstborn for my transgression, the fruit of my body for the sin of my soul? He has showed you, O man, what is good. And what does the LORD require of you? To act justly and to love mercy and to walk humbly with your God."

Jesus described the careful, time consuming activities of religious leaders, making sure they had paid the precise amount in their tithe, and then told them:

Matthew 23:23: "But you have neglected the more important matters of the law—justice, mercy and faithfulness."

The same blindness that drove the Saul of religion to be unjust, unmerciful and arrogant in his persecution of Christians is the same blindness at work in the religious leaders Jesus accused of neglecting justice, mercy and humility.

In our last chapter ("Blind Leading the Blind?) we recounted the interrogation to which the Judean temple authorities subjected the man whom Jesus cured of blindness. They did not believe Jesus capable of healing because they believed Jesus to be a lawbreaking sinner for "breaking" the Sabbath. For them, making sure that their holy day was not "broken" was far more important than a blind man being made whole.

When he was being given the third degree by the religious leaders the blind man argued:

John 9:32-33: *"Nobody has ever heard of opening the eyes of a man born blind. If this man were not from God, he could do nothing."*

The venomous response given to the formerly blind man by the religious leaders reveals how they despised those who failed to achieve the pinnacle of righteousness they felt they had achieved:

John 9:34: *"You were steeped in sin at birth; how dare you lecture us!"*

Blinded by religion, straining at a gnat and swallowing a camel (Matthew 23:24), these religious leaders assumed, based on religious appearances, that both Jesus and the blind man were sinners.

Christ-less religion blinds us to God's grace—legalism causes us to be unable to see what God's grace reveals, which is that *all* humans are in the same boat—we are *all* sinners (Romans 3:23). Sin is both an action and a condition of the human soul. When sin is an action it is a behavior that harms ourselves and/or others. Sins as actions arise out the fertile soil of the condition or state of sin. Sin is what humans do, it's an inevitable consequence of being human. For humans, sin goes with the territory. We *all* sin and we are *all* sinners. Sin is a part of the spiritual environment into which we are born —it defines the "territory" in which we live just as a driver's license or passport identifies our physical address. We live in the state of sin. Sin is just as much a part of our spiritual environment as air is part of the physical environment into which we are born.

The condition of sin in which we find ourselves is a disease—a soul-sick condition. Sin is the disease of human nature. To deny either sin as action or sin as a spiritual state is to say that Jesus died for nothing. Nowhere is this put more bluntly than in 1 John:

1 John 1:8, 10: "If we claim to be without sin, we deceive ourselves and the truth is not in us…. If we claim we have not sinned, we make him [God] out to be a liar and his word has no place in our lives (my edits)."

The most common human response to sin and the destruction it leaves in its wake is to try to fix it. Trying to fix sin by obeying moral laws is called legalism. Legalism is the foundation of Christ-less religion, the brick and mortar upon which the vast majority of religious corporations are constructed. Legalism is the belief that sin can be removed from our lives by our careful adherence to rules. Legalism further proposes that God's kingdom of heaven can be earned by good works. Some believe that their careful compliance with old covenant laws, like tithing, will convince God they are worthy of his kingdom.

When You Are Meticulous in the Minutia

Examine the spice rack of a good cook. Pull out a bottle of thyme, oregano or sage. Feel its weight. Are the spices heavy? Or is it the bottle that is heavy? Spices, as is obvious, weigh almost nothing. They are just leaves or crushed seeds.

Perhaps this is why Jesus chose everyday spices to make his point. Everyone who heard him speak that day knew what mint, dill and cumin looked like and tasted like. They all knew that the spices were leaves and seeds of miniscule weight. Many of those listening undoubtedly had these spices growing in pots at their homes.

Jesus was focusing on the practice, apparently widespread among some devout Jews, of carefully weighing the few handfuls of spices grown in one's personal little garden at home for the purpose of removing a tenth of the yield to take to the temple as a tithe. They were carefully obeying a text from the old covenant, as devoutly and literally as possible:

Leviticus 27:30: "A tithe of everything from the land, whether grain from the soil or fruit from the trees, belongs to the LORD; it is holy to the LORD."

In the fourth woe of Matthew 23, the signature passage for this chapter, Jesus describes a glaring example of hypocrisy—the painstaking tithing of a thimbleful of teeny leaves as practices by religious leaders—contrasting their obsession with incidentals with their massive failure in what was weighty and foundational: justice, mercy, and faithfulness.

Some attempt to put words into Jesus' mouth, ripping this statement by Jesus out of context, as if he agrees with mandatory, ten percent tithing imposed and required by some churches. While it is noteworthy that Jesus did not say that the teachers of the law and Pharisees were wrong for tithing spices (Matthew 23:23), we need to realize:

• **This passage does not mandate tithing.** In this passage Jesus bemoans incredible religious efforts to comply with the old covenant and what they so often lead to—completely missing the weighty and foundational essentials of the gospel.

• **This passage warns about legalism.** The larger context in which this passage appears is a stinging indictment by Jesus regarding the legalism of the religion of his day, a legalism fueled by their desire to do all they could do to be righteous under the terms of the old covenant.

• **Jesus was addressing the religious leaders of his day**. Jesus told them that they should tithe—just as they should avoid eating shrimp and pork and all kinds of old covenant stipulations. The new covenant had not yet fully come.

• **Tithing is not required for Christians**. The word "tithe" has an exact meaning. It means a requirement to give ten percent of your income. The new covenant does not require tithing, and thus it is erroneous for Christians to use the word "tithing" in connection with gifts given from the heart, freely and without compulsion.

Without Justice, Mercy and Faithfulness

In bondage to legalism, the religious leaders of Jesus' day were allowing rules to take precedence over people. A shepherd is supposed to care for the sheep, rather than making a career out of complaining and arguing about how flawed the sheep are. As Jesus said, "the Sabbath was made for man, not man for the Sabbath" (Mark 2:27). Regulations are made for people, not people for regulations. Again, Jesus sees that the religious leaders of his day had it backwards. Truly they had strained out a gnat and swallowed a camel.

What is the gnat they strained out? The little regulations that obsessed them. What is the camel? The resulting neglect of the weightier matters to God—specifically justice, mercy and faithfulness. What is the gnat they carefully obeyed and followed? Religion and all of its trivial pursuits.

What is the camel the religious leaders of Jesus' day swallowed, thereby ignoring the truly essential? The camel was their own blindness which plagued them, a blindness which caused them to ignore the very grace of God, personified, in their midst, by Jesus.

What a merciless game they played! Merciful leaders do not care more about the regulations than the people the regulations are supposed to help. You can get it right and still be wrong. You can believe that promiscuity is wrong, for example, but as a merciful parent do you disown your daughter or son when their hormones get the better of them? Caring more about the regulation than the person puts the cart before the horse. It kills relationship. Jesus could not sit by silently while the spiritual leaders of his nation equated God with their ugly art form of legalism.

In an attempt to be utterly faithful to regulations, the scribes and Pharisees became utterly unfaithful to the spiritual sheep they ostensibly served, and in so doing, unfaithful to their gracious, merciful and faithful God who loves sinful sheep and puts them before rules. Faithfulness is

101

understood within the context of relationship—being faithful means being faithful *to someone*.

Hypocrisy and the Parable of the Good Samaritan

We discussed the parable of the Good Samaritan in chapter one. The priest and the Levite knew the rules and kept them; they did not stop to check on a bloodied naked body on the side of the road to Jericho (Luke 10:25-37). Touching a corpse would have defiled them, and since the robbed man looked well and truly dead, they kept the rule by not stopping.

The religious leaders could not determine for sure whether the man who had been beaten and left for dead was a Jew. Many righteous Jews in Jesus' day interpreted the law in such a way that they were only under obligation to help a fellow Jew. Only fellow Jews were considered neighbors. Thus they asked Jesus for clarification.

Without his clothes—Jewish apparel—the priest and the Levite could not tell whether the robbed man was their neighbor, that is, a Jew. Perhaps the man was laying face down, on his belly, so there was no way to check his circumcision without rolling him over. Unable to tell whether the man was a Jew and whether he was dead, they were uncertain what legally correct action they should take. "The rules" said that you cannot come near a corpse or touch it, and you are under no obligation to assist a non-Jew. So they kept the rules and passed by. What a perfect example of putting rules before a person!

In Jesus' day, a high pedestrian bridge connected the upper city of Jerusalem to the temple. The upper city was the neighborhood where the upper-class wealthy lived, including priests, Sadducees, teachers of the law and Pharisees. One of the arches that supported this bridge, today called Wilson's Arch, exists intact near the Western Wall. The bridge once spanned the Tyropean Valley, where, below the bridge, the lower class worked, struggled and begged.

Picture the hypocritical, wealthy religious leaders,

dressed in clerical finery, clutching their precise tithe of spice leaves, crossing on their private bridge on their way to their church, the temple. And as they "went to church/temple"—leaving their well appointed homes, traveling to a magnificent temple, how many desperate people did they "walk over" on the streets below? Maybe that is why religious people had the bridge built in the first place: so they could walk to the temple and fulfill their obligations to the law without seeing or touching "sinners." After all, we can't let sinners get in the way of our religion, can we?

Hypocritical legalism often leads those it enslaves to police others, in a vain attempt to ensure that no one gets away with anything. Christ-less religion is characterized by zealous attempts to guarantee that everyone gets what they deserve.

Getting What We Deserve?

The dressing room door opens, and Karen walks out. She is just as beautiful as she was when I waited for her to walk down the aisle on a summer day in England just over 41 years ago. But, now, the summer of 2010, she is wearing a hospital-provided blue smock. As our eyes meet, the technicians say they are ready.

We walk through a massive, one-foot-thick steel door into the radiation chamber. It's a large room, about the size of a handball or squash court, dominated by the overwhelming presence of a Trilogy Linear Accelerator. The Trilogy is the state-of-the-art machine used by radiation oncologists to treat cancerous tumors with the most accurate radiation beams available.

I sit down and wait, as Karen inserts the mouth guard the dentist had fashioned. She takes her place on a long bench, and the technicians start to position her, finally fastening the custom made mask around her head and neck.

Sometimes, as I watch her being prepped for her treatment, I remember her as she was more than three decades ago—an involved, supportive mother of our now two adult children. Sometimes I visualize images, ingrained in my memory from old faded photos, of Karen as a little girl, long before I knew her, growing up on farms in Nebraska and Brazil, and finally in Longmont, Colorado. I imagine Karen skipping rope and playing hop-scotch, when she was the ages of Alexa and Kendall, our six and eight-year-old granddaughters. Whatever memory floods my mind when I watch her waiting for the treatment to begin, I always think, "she doesn't deserve this!"

I sit with her in the chamber until the machine is properly programmed, and then I leave the room along with the technicians. She is alone, the lights are dimmed, the soothing music Karen has chosen starts to play and the treatment begins. About ten minutes later her daily treatment is over, she is released from her mask, and returns to the dressing room. During the time when I wait for her, my mind often replays other past memories—each and every time, as I visualize her life and her contributions to the lives of others, I always think—"she doesn't deserve this!"

I can't tell you about my personal experiences with cancer surgery, or other treatments, such as chemotherapy or radiation. I can't tell you about an alternative treatment which cured me from cancer. I haven't personally had such experiences—yet. But I can talk about the pain of watching Karen, as she endures suffering.

During the months of May, June and July I watched, helplessly, as Karen experienced ever increasing levels of pain and suffering—all in a bid to "beat cancer." She fought the cancer and the painful side effects of radiation treatment while gamely celebrating Mothers' Day, Father's Day, our anniversary, my birthday, her birthday and the birthday of our nation. Sometimes she was barely able to talk. From the earliest stages of the treatment she had a hard time swallowing—even liquid. As the treatment has progressed, she needed to lie down and rest after the effort of "eating" her liquid meals.

I found myself joining all those who stand by, watching their loved ones suffer, wrestling with the question, "why?"

Karen has lived with me more than twice as long as she did with her now deceased parents. I presume I know Karen better than any other human does, and I can tell you that she didn't deserve what she was going through. I am the only other human being I know as well as I know Karen, and there is no doubt in my mind that I, of the two of us, deserve this kind of pain and suffering more than she does. I am not asking for such pain and suffering—I am simply saying that if God gives us what we deserve in this life, then I deserve the pain she endured more than she did. I'm not being noble, just truthful.

I can only conclude that we don't always deserve what we experience in this life. Life truly isn't fair, but then, did God ever tell us that it would be? In Luke 13:1-9 Jesus was asked about some who had been brutally killed by Pontius Pilate, and by way of response Jesus compared their death to that of 18 others who were victims of a freak accident, when a tower collapsed. Did either of these two groups of people who died get what they deserved—did they deserve what they got?

Then Jesus told them a parable about a man who had a fig tree planted in his vineyard—a fig tree that did not yield any fruit. The gardener wanted to cut down the fig tree, but the owner of the vineyard told the gardener to give the fig tree one more year. If getting what we deserve is the bottom line, then the barren fig tree deserved to be cut down. It was just taking up space and wasting the gardener's time. But Jesus depicts the landowner as giving the fig tree his grace and favor—*grace that is not deserved.* With the parable of the fig tree Jesus is driving our thinking away from cause and effect, and focusing our thoughts on God's richly undeserved grace.

Jesus repudiates ideas and notions that there is always a direct correlation between what happens to us and behavior, on our part, that may have caused it. The parable of the workers in the vineyard (Matthew 20:1-16) tells a story about those who worked hard and long, yet they did not receive any more pay than those who did not make the same effort.

Humanly, we are always concerned about what is fair. When someone receives a benefit we don't believe they deserve, we get upset and demand our rights.

Few things seem as unequal as the equal treatment of those we presume to be un-equals. Jesus explains that God is generous to everyone, because everything belongs to God. He asks those who are upset that others seem to be getting more than they deserve, "are you envious because I am generous?" (Matthew 20:15).

When Katrina hit New Orleans, many preachers were quick to point out that a gay rights parade/convention was being planned—they said God was punishing the Sodom and Gomorrah of New Orleans, and giving that notoriously sinful city what it deserved.

When an earthquake hit Northridge, California, some years ago, some preachers noted that Northridge was close to the California porn industry. The earthquake, according to them, was God's judgment, ensuring that the porn industry received what it deserved.

When Haiti suffered a devastating earthquake, some religious folks pointed to a long history of paganism and voodoo—Haiti was getting what it deserved.

In the aftermath of 9/11, two of the most well-known Christian television personalities/ministers in North America dogmatically claimed that God was punishing the United States for its tolerance of gays and lesbians. God was, they said, giving us what we deserved.

Do we deserve what we get? Do we get what we deserve?

I have held little babies who were born with AIDS—what did they do to deserve AIDS? Were children who were molested by priests getting what they deserved? Virtually every day we read of innocent men, women and children who, as a matter of time and chance, either die or are crippled by suicide bombings in Iraq and Afghanistan. Do civilians living in a war-torn area deserve to be maimed or blown up, more than you and I do? Do people living in Iran, Zimbabwe and North Korea deserve the inhumane conditions created by the despots who rule their countries? Is their suffering deserved by virtue of an "accident of birth"?

History books are filled with suffering—it's the curse of being human. Within the last 100 years, we have seen unspeakable atrocities—from a North American perspective the long list includes World War I and II, Korea, Vietnam, Iraq and Afghanistan. Then there's Bosnia, Angola, Sudan, Zimbabwe, Uganda and Rwanda. The killing fields of Cambodia, the massacres in Bosnia. There's a rogue's gallery of mass murderers—Stalin, Lenin, Idi Amin, Pol Pot and Sadam Hussein. And there's the Holocaust—the evil cloud that hangs over the 20th century—described by Marvin Hier, the Founder and Dean of the Simon Wiesenthal Center, as "the total eclipse of humanity."

The Epitome of Un-Grace

There are those, as you know, who say that the Jews deserved the Holocaust. I absolutely reject that insane notion. There are also those who say that billions of people will be slow roasted, for all eternity, tortured in hell, condemned by God because they didn't measure up to his standards. I absolutely reject than notion as the epitome of un-grace.

Preachers fulminate about those who will get eternal torture (what they deserve) because they weren't baptized with the right amount of water at the right age by the right religious authority using the right religious creed. Many will suffer eternal torment, according to some religious authorities, because they never said the sinner's prayer, because they weren't confirmed, because they never gave their heart to the Lord, because they didn't accept an invitation to join a church, because they don't pay tithes…or whatever. While I believe in judgment, I reject the idea of a God of wrath and vengeance exacting eternal torture on those who failed to perform at a high enough religious standard, or, beyond that, exacting eternal torture on those who never seemingly even had a chance to know God.

Call me a heretic, but the God I worship and adore is being hideously misrepresented by religious professionals who hold the club of eternal torture in hell over the heads of their fear and anxiety-ridden followers.

I know that many within Christendom are going to respond: "So, you don't believe in the holy God of justice and the richly deserved suffering and curses he imposes?" My response: "I don't believe in your definition of God, but I can tell you about the God I know, who is a God of mercy, grace and love. Even then, I cannot tell you all about the God I know, because neither I, nor anyone else, regardless of how loud they may yell, how many religious stripes they have on their uniform or how many degrees they have, can tell you all there is to know about the majesty and mystery of God."

Do we get what we deserve? While there are many times when we suffer consequences of our actions, when all of our behaviors are considered, God does not give us what we actually deserve. There are times when we are victims of time and chance. Disease, accident and violence all happen. The sun rises and sets on "good" people and evil people, God "sends rain on the righteous and the unrighteous" (Matthew 5:45). But even when we factor in accidents and time and chance, we still don't pay all the penalties we deserve.

As God's children we suffer— suffering is part of what it means to be a Christian (1 Peter:2:21). We have no guarantee of immunity from the corruption and heartache of the world in which we live. Jesus didn't claim any such immunity when he lived among us as one of us. We don't have much control over what happens to us, but by God's grace, we can determine how we will respond to what we experience.

Do we get what we deserve, in the sense of *karma*? Is God in heaven supervising an equal distribution of cause and effect, making all things balance in the scales of justice? No, he has offered no such promise. When bad things happen to us, trying to find some secret or long forgotten sin for which God is now cursing us is a fool's errand. Such thinking is primitive, mystical superstition. It is, at its very foundation, the embodiment of un-grace. As outlaw William Munny (Clint Eastwood's character in the film *Unforgiven*) says: "Deserve's got nothing to do with it."

I can tell you about the one thing that no one deserves. No one. It's called grace. No one deserves it. God's generosity. The gift of his lavish love, and of his unconditional forgiveness. We don't deserve his grace. God's grace cannot be purchased with meritorious deeds. It can only be received, as a gift.

God's grace defies logic and offends our sense of fair play. We like his grace when we know we need it, but we are scandalized when others whom we feel to be unworthy also receive it. We don't deserve the cross of Christ—but it's offered to us all, by God's grace.

I don't fully understand all the reasons for pain and heartache. I don't understand the suffering of those who do not, from my perspective, deserve it. But most of all, I will never, ever, on this side of eternity, understand why we deserve God's grace. Because of Jesus, God, in his grace, chooses to determine us as being worthy of his love and grace.

I thank God that he has given us what we do not deserve.

The Failure of Religion

Christ-less religion, which is founded on legalism, fails at justice, mercy and faithfulness. Legalistic religion puts rules before people, presuming to itself the roles of judge, jury and executioner. Hypocritical legalism strains out gnats while swallowing camels—it majors in the minutia. Hypocritical legalism drives its followers to ensure others get what they deserve. The un-grace of religion is such a contrast with God's grace, it raises an interesting question: What if God were to put rules before people? Thank God for his grace. Thank God we have an advocate, Jesus Christ, who ensures that we do not receive what we would otherwise deserve.

If God were primarily interested in balancing the scales of justice, ensuring that each one of us receives exactly what we deserve, he never would have, in the person of Jesus, joined us in human flesh (his birth—the incarnation). Had God's primary focus been each one of us getting what we deserve, he never would have sacrificed himself for our sin (his cross, his atoning work on our behalf), and he never would have destroyed death and the grave (his resurrection). If God were more concerned with recording all of our sins so that we receive all of the punishment we deserve, he certainly would never come to live his life in us, because after all, you cannot help a bunch of rule-breakers!

If the rules were more important to God than people, he would enforce the rules, period. We would still be hopeless slaves of rules we cannot keep. Why would a God who cares more about rules than people ever come to liberate us from the rules? A legalistic God would not become one of us and die to save us from condemnation under the rules. Such a God, like the Pharisees Jesus criticizes, would nitpick and condemn. Such a God would be an abusive, perhaps even emotionally unbalanced shepherd who beats the sheep just for being sheep.

Our Prayer: Lord, we nitpick and blame, we obsess on minutia, and we neglect our need for love and our call to love. Have mercy on us sinners. Give us transformed hearts—live in us Jesus so that you might be, in and through us, just, merciful, and faithful to others. Thank you for giving us of the riches of your grace—thank you for giving us what we can never deserve.

Chapter 7

Might As Well Put Lipstick on a Pig

"Woe to you, teachers of the law and Pharisees, you hypocrites! You clean the outside of the cup and dish, but inside they are full of greed and self-indulgence. Blind Pharisee! First clean the inside of the cup and dish, and then the outside also will be clean. Woe to you, teachers of the law and Pharisees, you hypocrites! You are like whitewashed tombs, which look beautiful on the outside but on the inside are full of dead men's bones and everything unclean. In the same way, on the outside you appear to people as righteous but on the inside you are full of hypocrisy and wickedness."—Matthew 23:25-28

Movies, especially when shown in a theatre, are considered evil by conservative Muslims. For the last 30 years fundamentalist Muslims have banned movie theatres in Saudi Arabia. But on weekends and religious holidays, the highway to Bahrain, a neighboring country which hosts ultra-modern cinema complexes, is choked with vehicles, particularly with young Saudis and their families. Reports indicate that almost 100,000 people travel hundreds of miles each weekend and on holidays to Bahrain for the purpose of watching movies on the large screen, forbidden in the kingdom of Saudi Arabia.

A Saudi newspaper investigated this phenomenon, discovering the paradox that some of the most vocal critics of cinema complexes in Saudi Arabia can be regularly found enjoying movies in Bahrain. Religion and its dictates turn those it enslaves into two-faced pretenders.

The religious brand name is beside the point. Legalistic religion, marching under any flag or banner, causes its followers to take extreme measures, so that they can, by compliance with religious dictates, appear righteous. The unreasonable pronouncements and directives of their religion turns its followers into hypocrites.

In the **fifth and sixth woes** of Matthew 23 Jesus likens the teachers of the law and Pharisees to 1) eating utensils which are superficially clean, having been washed only on the visible surface, and 2) tombs whose exteriors are well maintained, but internally are filled with unseen decomposing bodies. The signature verses for this chapter condemn hypocritical religious authorities who are two-faced actors focused on exteriors—looking clean, looking alive and looking righteous. The teachers of the law and Pharisees dutifully projected a righteous image. They seemed convinced that the way to become clean, alive and righteous was to strive to look clean, alive and righteous. Therein lies their spiritual blindness. And therein lies the lie of religion.

If only the outside of a cup is clean, then the cup is of no use. A tomb may be whitewashed, but it is still a tomb. A contemporary idiom conveys a similar message—"you can put lipstick on a pig, but a pig is still a pig." Religious attempts to produce surface beauty are truly only skin deep. "Blind Pharisee!" Jesus exclaimed. He was exposing the lie: *Cleaning up your act doesn't clean up your heart.* In the last chapter we learned about hypocrisy—claiming to be someone or something one is not. In this chapter we will explore the inevitable result of hypocrisy—a preoccupation with how we appear to others.

When Faith Is Based on Surface Attraction

Having already exposed their hypocrisy concerning broader phylacteries and longer tassels and places of honor at banquets and their efforts to exalt themselves at the expense of those they pretended to serve, you would think that Jesus had said enough on the subject of the pride and vanity of religious appearances. But Jesus digs to the heart of the matter. Will we fall for the idea that we can be admired for what we appear to be, or will we seek the internal beauty of a changed heart, made available by God's grace?

Do you see the astounding implication of what Jesus is saying? Slaving in a salt mine endlessly trying to please religious taskmasters is only one of the curses of Christ-less religion. Fruitless, never-ending self-salvation programs promoted and pushed by religion are a curse. But there is another debilitating curse produced by legalism—Christ-less religion turns its captives into emotional and spiritual cripples.

The cup of empty religion and the tomb of dead religion shine and sparkle externally, but internally they are filled with waste matter and death. The apparently clean cup and the whitewashed tomb are façades, offering false promises. The glitter of Christ-less religion is not gold—it's fool's gold.

Christ-less religion is an insatiable master, damning its captives to a lifetime of efforts that are never good enough. Those who are duped by the religious quest for admiration are chasing the proverbial pot of gold at the end of the rainbow. The quest for admiration turns many religious captives into zombies who are incapable of letting either God or fellow humans love them. A preoccupation with one's own spiritual appearance actually prevents real, lasting relationships—with God or humanity at large. A preoccupation with spiritual appearances can cause extraordinary behavior—condemning cinema complexes in one's own neighborhood, while traveling hundreds of miles to attend a movie in a cinema complex in another country!

Jesus' instruction to the Pharisees to clean the inside of the cup is far from just another religious self-help program. Jesus' call to clean the inside of the cup is a call to let the light of Jesus shine on the dark places of our souls and allow our hearts to be washed with the living water of life—no matter how terrifying that process may seem, and no matter how painful it might be.

The quest for admiration via outward appearances is actually a denial of grace. God welcomes us to experience his grace by inviting us: "Let me love you." But before we can accept this invitation we must become vulnerable, trusting God. Allowing love to penetrate our hearts, whether that love is human or divine in origin, involves a risk on our part.

Matthew 18:3-4: "...Unless you change, and become like little children, you will never enter the kingdom of heaven. Therefore, whoever humbles himself like this child is the greatest in the kingdom of heaven."

The change about which Jesus spoke is, of course, the transformation of spiritual rebirth. This spiritual transformation cannot take place as a product of human effort, but, on the other hand, it will not take place without human consent. Consent for new birth is evidenced by surrender to Jesus, and the humility of accepting dependence on God and his grace as the foundation of spiritual life.

The spiritual pride produced by their religious efforts blinded the Pharisees from seeing any need of receiving God's love by his grace, for they felt they had already obtained his favor by their works. Their spiritual pride prevented them from humbling themselves, like a child, and accepting God's love—their pride caused them to run from God's love. The prodigious religious efforts of the Pharisees, aimed at pleasing God on the basis of their performance, actually insulated and fortified them against God's grace.

Religion creates an alternative spiritual reality—a delusion—so that its followers believe a lie. Christ-less religion has a voracious, unquenchable appetite, causing its followers to relentlessly seek admiration for their religious accomplishments. Belief in the false claims of the mirage of religion can ultimately devour and destroy the potential for a positive response to God's grace. Religion blinded the teachers of the law and the Pharisees so that they were unable to see their pathetic state—just as it continues to do so for hundreds of millions today. Religious striving turned their lives into a loveless lie. Spiritually they were but an empty shell, dying from the inside out.

Covering Our Shame and Guilt

"Poppa, put this dress on—and these shoes." Emerson, our youngest grandchild, was two and one-half years old at the time. She was enjoying (but not as much as we were!) a "sleep-over" at our house and she wanted me to play Barbies with her. Perhaps she felt I needed to discover my feminine side, because she assigned me the task of dressing her two Barbies in the outfits she selected. Emerson was incredibly patient with me as I fumbled with flimsy material and Velcro fasteners. As I obediently followed her whimsical dictates, endlessly dressing and undressing and redressing the two Barbies, I started to think of Adam and Eve. God created them just like Barbie dolls—in their birthday suits, *au natural.*

The first religious behavior in which our ancient parents participated was "dressing up." After spurning God's teaching and rejecting his grace, their shame and guilt motivated them to cover up and hide from God. They did the very thing Jesus chided the scribes and Pharisees for doing—cleaning only the outside, whitewashing the tomb of death.

Have you ever thought about what happens when Barbie and Ken (the male companion for Barbie) "join" a church? They are given a membership kit filled with exercises, rituals, behaviors, practices and religious outfits expressly designed to cover their shame and guilt. Because Christless religion is based on making us "look good" the real need of connecting with God is often overlooked. The entire exercise of "church" often becomes a futile attempt for humans to paper over the cracks of their internal shame and guilt. But, the only way our shame and guilt can be washed clean is through the transformation of our hearts which we receive from God, by his grace, via a spiritual re-birth.

Shame is realized, in our culture, when we fail to measure up to standards set by our 1) parents, 2) society at large and 3) religion.

115

Overbearing parents use shame as a method of control and punishment: "You ought to be ashamed of yourself!" Shame results when we fail to please our parents. Children who must experience and endure overbearing parents are given a warped idea of love.

Society at large worships those who look good and who attain wealth and status. Shame results when we fail to measure up to the high standards of society. Society at large loves the beautiful and the talented and the wealthy—leaving the vast majority condemned as unloved, some even considered to be un-loveable.

Christ-less religion heaps shame on those who fail to measure up to its standards, and in the name of God pronounces those who fail to achieve as unworthy. Religion perverts God's love—giving us the idea that God loves only those who produce—only those who please and appease him.

There is nothing that we humans need more desperately than God's love. We are hungry for his love. Because we have been exposed to wrong-headed religiously inspired notions about God's love, we are easy prey for "get-loved-quick" schemes. As a result we often wind up looking for God's love in all the wrong places. While we fear that God will never love us, we also fear making ourselves vulnerable to him. As a result of having been pronounced "losers" by the games religion plays, we are easily convinced that we just need to try harder. When we are seduced and deceived we really believe that dressing and covering up with spiritual facades will earn us God's love—but all we earn is the cotton candy of religious approval and admiration.

God's Love—Tough and Relentless

Jesus sent a message of tough love to the church in Laodicea (Revelation 3:14-21). He said he rebukes and disciplines those whom he loves. He loved Laodicea enough to tell them the truth about their true, internal spiritual condition. They were deceived by spiritual glitter, failing to realize that all that glitters is not gold. They believed the lie that cleaning up their act (by trying to improve their spiritual appearance) would clean up their heart. Their best efforts amounted to lipstick on pigs wallowing in the swill of the barnyard.

The Laodiceans were deluded—blind to their lukewarm hearts, blind to their poverty, nakedness and wretchedness of spirit. The malaise—the spiritually dysfunctional perspective evidenced by the church in Laodicea is still wreaking havoc today. The original Laodiceans were hiding behind the wealth and finery of what seemed to them to be spiritually bedazzling Ken and Barbie outfits, and in so doing they shut out true riches—the riches of God's love. They shut out and rejected God's love in favor of religious appearances. God's love was knocking on the door, but they rejected his overtures, leaving God's grace and love on the outside, looking in.

Revelation 3:14-22: "To the angel of the church in Laodicea write: These are the words of the Amen, the faithful and true witness, the ruler of God's creation. I know your deeds, that you are neither cold nor hot. I wish you were either one or the other! So, because you are lukewarm—neither hot nor cold— I am about to spit you out of my mouth. You say, 'I am rich; I have acquired wealth and do not need a thing.' But you do not realize that you are wretched, pitiful, poor, blind and naked. I counsel you to buy from me gold refined in the fire, so you can become rich; and white clothes to wear, so you can cover your shameful nakedness; and salve to put on your eyes, so you can see. Those whom I love I rebuke and discipline. So be earnest, and repent. Here I am! I stand at the door and knock. If anyone hears my voice and opens the door, I will come in and eat with him, and he with me. To him who overcomes, I will give the right to sit with me on my throne, just as I overcame and sat down with my Father on his throne. He who has an ear, let him hear what the Spirit says to the churches (my emphasis). "

Jesus is speaking of his burning, passionate love as the refining fire. The pure gold of which he speaks is a heart that God is burning clean of impurities so his love can flow through it. The refined gold Jesus mentions can only be given by God's grace. The true spiritual riches all belong to God, and apart from him we have no resources to purchase them. The good news is that we are invited to accept the fact that Jesus bought and paid for us on his cross. If we surrender to God's grace, if we trust him and accept his invitation to let him love us, then our hearts can be transformed, a spiritual exchange ("such a deal") that Revelation describes as "buying" gold refined by fire. Jesus said to the Pharisees:

Luke 16:15: *"You are the ones who justify yourselves in the eyes of men, but God knows your hearts. What is highly valued among men is detestable in God's sight."*

The impurity of the human heart was no news flash to these religious leaders. It was a major theme of the Old Testament. Jesus was reiterating a truth they already knew:

1 **Samuel** 16:7: *"The LORD does not look at the things man looks at. Man looks at the outward appearance, but the LORD looks at the heart."*

God's Love Is a Consuming Fire

The false, idolatrous heart seeks to "please men" by creating a false self to earn human approval and admiration. This is what Jesus means by cleaning only the outside of the cup. This is a false, idolatrous worship of appearances. The Lord bypasses appearances, however, and goes straight for the heart. George MacDonald, a mentor and friend of C.S. Lewis, clarifies:

> "Nothing is inexorable but love...for love loves unto purity.... Therefore all that is not beautiful in the beloved, all that comes between and is not of love's kind, must be destroyed. And our God is a consuming fire...." (C.S.Lewis *George MacDonald. An Anthology*, Macmillan Publishing Co., Inc., New York, 1978)

The refining fire of God's love is all about burning out religious impurities which adulterate God's amazing grace. God's love and grace is "tough" for humans because we are hard wired to perform and work and earn and achieve—and religion uses this innate sense of hard work in such a way that it places its followers in absolute opposition to God's grace.

The transforming, spiritual purification which a Christian experiences, in and through Christ, is neither a Spartan series of legalistic hoops one must jump through nor is it an academic examination of biblical knowledge that one must successfully pass before God grants entrance into the kingdom of heaven.

A refiner's fire purifies and redeems. Jesus is that refiner's fire. He is the personification of God's love—he is a burning bliss. The goal of the refiner's fire is unadulterated truth and unconditional love—the uncontaminated riches of God's grace. What is our response to this gracious fire of God's love? God's pure, radical grace may scare the hell out of us, but if we invite it into our lives it will be like a refiner's fire, purifying our hearts. God's grace will consume all of the religious justifications we drape over our Ken and Barbie dolls in a futile attempt to hide from God, and cover up our shame and guilt.

Because we are scared of being spiritually naked before God, as were Adam and Eve, our first instinct is to "do something religious" in a vain attempt to cover ourselves. In so doing we forget the clear instruction of Scripture, which tells us that the only adequate covering we can ever have is given to us by God's grace, through Jesus' perfect work on his cross.

Sadly, the oh-so-human response to God's love is to run away, to hide behind facades, and to build fortresses of human admiration. But the good news is that God's burning love will not go away. Religious fig leaves will not deter God from pursuing us. God loves us even though we run away from him and even though religion confuses us. God loves us in spite of our attempts to cover ourselves in religious outfits, displaying our unique and superior denominational doctrines that we believe make us "better" than others. But denominational doctrines have their price!

119

I'm reminded of the story about a woman whose beloved dog had just died, so she called her Baptist minister to see if he would officiate at a funeral. The pastor said, "I'm sorry, but I can't do that. We Baptists don't believe in funerals for dogs. But I know that the Anglican church down the road has a special annual service for the blessing of animals—and they actually ask people to bring their pets to church for a blessing. Can you believe that? Anyway, you might call the Anglican priest and see if he would officiate at the funeral you want to have for your dog."

The woman responded, "All right. You are my pastor, and I was hoping you would officiate, but I'll call the Anglican priest. By the way, can you give me some advice? How much should I pay him? I was thinking $500 wouldn't be enough—should I pay him $1,000?" After a long pause the pastor said, "You know, I was just thinking, your dog was baptized as a Baptist, wasn't he?"

Love or Torture?

God is our heavenly Father, and he "disciplines us for our good" (Hebrews 12:10). But many fail, given their oh-so-imperfect experiences with earthly parents, to comprehend the way that God loves us. God is not an abusive God! Many within the world of Christendom would have us believe that the Jesus who preached love, even for our enemies—the Jesus who came to reveal the Father, the Jesus who himself was God in the flesh—that same Jesus, we are told, satisfied the wrath of the Father on his cross. The basic assumption, shared by many Christians, is that Jesus took our place, and got the hell beat out of him by an angry God whom our sins had offended.

Because Christ-less religion cannot exist without an agitated God, it has created, in its own image, a God of wrath and anger. The cross of Christ is thus explained as the necessary bloodletting which satisfied the Father, who had been offended by sin and had to be appeased.

Big business religion has perpetrated the delusion (false appearance) of a God of wrath by replacing God with its religious legalisms rather than faithfully representing the one true God. Pop theology has encouraged the illusion of an angry God who must be appeased because such a concept serves the purposes of religious institutionalism—specifically the control it must maintain over its followers. Thus we have the Father seeking punitive vengeance for the sins of the world (which would include you and me) and "taking it out" on the Son, so that we might be "saved."

That's one of the major reasons I object to the abuse of the word "saved" as an evangelical Christian cliché. In popular usage, the word is filled with the baggage of an angry God from whom we must be "saved." If we accept this notion, then somehow, in a way that is never really explained, the one God who is Father, Son and Holy Spirit, divides on this issue. The Father is really upset and wants payback—the Son is compassionate and finally persuades his Father to let him take the fall in our stead. The Son saves us from the Father! How twisted is that?

When institutionalized religion hijacked and confiscated the gospel for its own self-serving purposes, it used its contrivances about eternal torture in the afterlife to control people. The hell of Christendom at large not only subdues and enslaves its followers, it is used to give perverse pleasure about the ghastly, grotesque and gruesome nightmare awaiting those outside of the pseudo salvation (fire insurance) offered by Christ-less religion.

According to this popular notion, what exactly are we "saved" from? Eternal torment in the hottest kind of hell imaginable, where we are dispatched (by the Father) to Satan so that we can be fiendishly tortured, forever and ever! Religion presumes to save us from a hell that is largely of its own making, a fabricated hell it needs to survive. Christ-less religion, as it devises fiendish punishment which awaits us if we don't get with the program, is somewhat like the old snake-oil healer.

You remember those old movies depicting life in the frontier days? The traveling medicine show rolled into town, and the old snake-oil healer tried to convince would-be customers that they have a mysterious, incurable illness. Once the listeners believed the con, hoping their health problems could be cured, they paid the price and the wonder-working snake-oil salesman applied the mysterious lotion/oil, pronouncing the illness to be miraculously healed! In a similar way, Christ-less religion deludes us into believing it will save us, with its get-out-of-hell free kind of salvation, but it's all smoke and mirrors! God's grace, on the other hand, offers us real salvation, the *setting-us-free-from-religion kind of salvation.*

The gospel of Jesus Christ is clear. God offers his love to all humanity, and offers all humanity a choice. The gospel is not clear about how and when God makes that offer, and what exactly constitutes an offer on his part and a refusal or rejection on the part of humans. Christ-less religion speculates that many will never hear of God's offer and thus be condemned to eternal torture. So, many churches unabashedly and dogmatically tell their congregations, "unless you get busy and tell the unsaved about God's offer to stay out of hell, then it will be your fault if they wind up there." Christ-less religion heaps shame and guilt on those who fail to "witness" to people who might have otherwise been "saved" from God's anger. How far from God's grace can religion get?

If God's love is offered to anyone, it is offered to everyone. Everyone—whether individual or corporate groups and gatherings of Christians are aware of how, exactly, God is offering his love and relationship to "others" or not! God offers us his love, but he doesn't tell us that he will inform us about each and every way and time and circumstance when he offers his love to others. Don't you think it's strange that Christianity has been so warped and twisted by religion that many church-goers think that when they do good things God will reward them and when they behave badly God will punish them? How twisted is that? Everything Jesus said and did reveals a loving God, rather than the agitated, punitive God pushed by religion.

What does our loving God do with those who reject his

love? Knowing the gospel of Jesus Christ and experiencing the love of God, how can we believe religious myths that God will ensure, in some way, that either he or the devil (in some versions, both!?) will inflict eternal, unbearable physical pain on the unfortunate souls who wind up in hell?

The details of heaven and hell are not provided in the Bible, and therefore extreme caution is advised when speculating about either. We do know, however, that God's tough love is all about the very nature of God and his no-matter-what love. We do know that God's love has no boundaries. Ponder the thoughts of Peter Kreeft:

"The very fires of Hell are the love and joy of God experienced as wrath and torment by the soul that hates the light and its purifying fire.... Though the damned do not love God, God loves them, and this is their torture. (*Everything You Ever Wanted to Know About Heaven: But Never Dreamed of Asking!* By Peter Kreeft, pp. 206, 234.)

Escaping From the Delusion of Religion— Only the First Step

The Exodus from Egypt is the foundation of the Old Testament story of the people of God. The major themes of our relationship with God, fully revealed by God's grace in and through Jesus Christ—escape and salvation from spiritual captivity, an unblemished lamb sacrificed on our behalf and transformation and new life, by grace rather than works— are central to the Exodus and Passover story.

The children of Israel left the physical and spiritual captivity of Egypt—they had to get out so that they could worship God. It's a story which has been repeated in many eras and generations. In Germany, Martin Luther had to leave the Roman Catholic church, with all of its corruption, so that he could be a Christian. But rejecting the un-grace of oppressive, authoritarian religion is just the first step. If God's grace is not embraced by spiritual refugees, they usually wind up exchanging one delusion for another.

Later, in England, the Puritans wanted to continue Luther's Reformation, believing that the Reformation had stopped short of achieving its purposes (especially in England). Because the Church of England controlled all visible forms of Christian expression in England, the Puritans became convinced that they had to leave England. They were convinced that the Church of England and its authority was hopelessly corrupt, so they came to "New" England so that they might worship God in freedom. In their case, they had to leave the Church of England as well as the nation, so they could freely practice their faith.

But the lie of religion is like (with my apologies to the canine world) fleas on a dog. It's difficult to "shake" religion. Changing the metaphor, religion can also be compared to a hallucinogenic delusion-inducing drug to which hundreds of millions have become addicted.

The children of Israel found it difficult to live with the freedom God gave them, they couldn't "shake" all their religious fleas, nor could they "kick" the religious habit, so they soon returned to the gods of their captivity in Egypt, welcoming the golden calf that Aaron fashioned for them (Exodus 32:16).

Rejecting the hierarchical abuse of the church of England, the Puritans soon fashioned their own institutionalized, rigorous legalism—it wasn't long before they were persecuting others just as they themselves had once been persecuted. They established strict codes of behavior and morality, enforcing them with stern, hell-fire-and-brimstone threats of eternal punishment for those who failed to conform.

The Puritans struggled to "purify" the rituals and ceremonies of Christendom which they believed had polluted their faith. But their draconian endeavors to be "better" Christians wound up on the same garbage dump as all other human contrivances aimed at earning God's love. The Puritan answer was to leave "old" England for "New" England. But because God's grace was not their foundation, their answer was merely a "new" legalism, just another religious prescription based on humanly produced righteousness.

The Puritans proved to be just one more chapter in the history of deluded, hypocritical, legalistic religion. They rightly identified a toxic form of religion, and rejected it, but their spiritual blindness caused them to focus on the outside of the cup. The Puritans rejected one spiritually unhealthy religion, but in their failure to fully embrace God's grace, they just changed the brand of lipstick they were putting on the pig.

Like all other ventures which attempt to climb higher and get closer to God than anyone has before, Puritanism failed, because the yardstick by which they measured their success was based on human performance. Their goal was to create a better spiritual world than the one they experienced within the Church of England, but in the end they simply created an appearance, so that their illusion of spirituality caused them to move deeper into the swamplands of bad news religion.

Religion at large is a lie because it misrepresents God, turning him into the very opposite of the love that he is, and the grace by which he conveys and shares that love. Christless religion offers you a damnable alternative. Get out the religious Barbie dolls. Dress up. Cover up. Put on the outfits religion supplies you. Wear your religious mask. Hide behind your spiritual façade. Counterfeit grace and replace it with religious performance. Bypass true righteousness, which comes only by God's grace, by trying to look righteous.

Humans will always admire external appearances they can see, more than the inner, invisible grace of God. But God is not fooled by "dress up" games—he does not look on outward appearances, but looks instead on the heart.

Saved From the Façade of Religion by God's Consuming Love

1 John 4:9-10: "This is how God showed his love among us: He sent his one and only Son into the world that we might live through him. This is love, not that we loved God, but that he loved us and sent his Son as an atoning sacrifice for our sins."

The fire of God's love is demonstrated to us by his cross. You might say that the cross of Christ is God's own crucible (a melting pot for metals in a refinery)—thus the refiner's fire of God's love and grace is the cross of Christ. Our relationship with God is based on what he has done for us—not what we can do for him. Dump the religion. Trust God and run to him. Reject the façade of religion—embrace grace!

Our Prayer:

Lord, why do we run from you? Why do we fear the one thing that will bring us life? Why are we afraid to step into the light and take an honest look at the ugliness that lives within our hearts? Help us see the futility and silliness of thinking that our external actions will clean up our hearts. Cleaning up our act will not clean up our heart. Our heart can only be cleansed by your grace. Create in us clean hearts, O God, and renew right spirits within us. Test us. Refine us. Purify us. Consume everything within our hearts that is not your own love.

Chapter 8

Religion Gone Wild

"Woe to you, teachers of the law and Pharisees, you hypocrites! You build tombs for the prophets and decorate the graves of the righteous. And you say, 'If we had lived in the days of our forefathers, we would not have taken part with them in shedding the blood of the prophets. So you testify against yourselves that you are the descendents of those who murdered the prophets. Fill up, then, the measure of the sin of your forefathers! You snakes! You brood of vipers! How will you escape being condemned to hell? Therefore I am sending you prophets and wise men and teachers. Some of them you will kill and crucify; others you will flog in your synagogues and pursue from town to town. And so upon you will come all the righteous blood that has been shed on earth, from the blood of righteous Abel to the blood of Zechariah son of Berekiah, whom you murdered between the temple and the altar. I tell you the truth, all this will come upon this generation."—Matthew 23:29-36

Don't ever take candy from a stranger—he may want to hurt you! Being suspicious of strangers is one of the most important lessons parents impart to children. But the task of warning and equipping children about the potential of abuse from those they know and trust is a daunting task. Regardless of our age, being violated by someone who occupies a position of trust is one of the most painful and bitter experiences of our lives.

Sexual, emotional, verbal, financial and even violent behavior perpetrated by religion and its authorities are usually traumatic, never-to-be-forgotten experiences. Victims of religious abuse encounter long term consequences, especially in terms of their relationship with God. As he concludes his sermon in Matthew 23, Jesus addresses the shameless, flagrant brutality and savagery of Christ-less religion.

Jesus' **seventh and last woe** may be the harshest of them all. He calls these religious tyrants *hypocrites and snakes, children of murderers who themselves flog and crucify God's true prophets and wise men and teachers.* No pulled punches here. In the previous two chapters we saw the hypocritical façade of Christ-less religion. In this chapter Jesus unmasks religion to expose it as the hideous, repulsive predator it really is.

The final sermon of Jesus' earthly ministry is almost over. In the metaphor of running a race, Jesus is rounding the final turn and heading for the wire. And what a conclusion! Jesus, as he wraps up this sermon, is turning his gaze on things to come. He is not just condemning the religious leaders and their ancestors for their treatment of those whom God sent to Jerusalem. He is prophesying the oh-so-soon torture and crucifixion to which they will subject him.

Jesus lets these religious leaders know that he is well aware of their murderous plan to kill him, and he places their plan for him in the context of Jerusalem's historical pattern of abusing those whom God sent to her. These religious professionals are not just blind and hypocritical. They are dangerous.

Jesus wanted everyone who heard his sermon at the Jerusalem temple that day to realize the perverse consequences that can happen when anyone dares to get in the way of the religious industry. Religious leaders can resemble poisonous vipers coiled to strike.

The passage that explains this final woe contains a phrase, with eleven stinging words, that provides an excellent introduction to our discussion of religion gone wild.

Matthew 23:32: "Fill up, then, the measure of the sin of your forefathers!"

To further grasp Jesus' meaning, look at these two translations of the same verse.

New Living Translation: "Go ahead and finish what your ancestors started."
New Jerusalem Bible: "Very well then, finish off the work that your ancestors began."

With bitter irony, Jesus gave voice to the unspoken, death-dealing brutality that results when the ugly truth of religion is unmasked—hell hath no fury like religion when it is exposed! Jesus lays down the gauntlet, telling religious leaders to just keep on doing what they have always done. "Oppose God. Kill his messengers. Kill me. You are sons of snakes, so go ahead and do what snakes do—strike and kill."

It should be obvious, but for clarity let's state the obvious. The Jewish religion had no monopoly on brutalizing God's messengers. Bloodthirsty brutality experienced by those who oppose religion is a recurring theme throughout church history. The history of Christendom is filled with examples of religion gone wild. The Crusades and the Spanish Inquisition are well-known examples. The so-called "Geneva experiment" that gave rise to what we know as Calvinism today is yet another example of what happens to those who get in the way of religious agendas. The Salem Witch Trials in New England, fueled by the religion of the Puritans, is yet another historical example of religion gone wild.

The Religion Headquartered in Jerusalem Killed Prophets?

Was there really a pattern in history of Judean religious authorities killing prophets? Jesus' indictment of religious leaders as murderers is shocking, and perhaps for that reason some try to scurry around to find a way to deny the charge—perhaps they are trying to take the heat off religion! Some claim that the Old Testament names very few prophets who were killed in Jerusalem (just two to be specific), plus one more who had a close scrape.

In response to those who doubt that there was a pattern of killing prophets in Jerusalem, here are five reasons to believe it was true.

1) There are Old Testament references to the evil done in Jerusalem by its leaders and their spilling of innocent blood (2 Kings 21:16; Isaiah 3:8-9, 4:4; Jeremiah 13:26-27; Micah 3:9-10).

2) There are many biblical verses that refer to the disdain for and mistreatment of prophets—Jeremiah is but one example (Jeremiah 20:2, 37:15-21, 38:6-16).

3) There are Old Testament verses that refer to unnamed prophets being killed. Just because these prophets are not named and their deaths are not specifically described does not negate the Old Testament claim that this happened many times (1 Kings 19:10; Nehemiah 9:26; Jeremiah 2:30).

4) There are two Old Testament references regarding prophets by the names of Zechariah and Uriah as having been killed in Jerusalem. The first was stoned (2 Chronicles 24:20-21) and the second was struck down with a sword (Jeremiah 26:20-23).

5) The New Testament also affirms that Jerusalem had a history of killing prophets. The New Testament writers not only record the violent reaction of the Jewish religion to the growth of early Christianity, but they confirm historical examples of religious brutalities in the Old Testament:

Luke 13:34: "O Jerusalem, Jerusalem, you who kill the prophets and stone those sent to you...."

*1 **Thessalonians** 2:14-15: "You suffered from your own countrymen the same things those churches suffered from the Jews [Judean authorities], who killed the Lord Jesus and the prophets and also drove us out"* (my edits).

Hebrews 11:36-38: "Some [prophets] faced jeers and flogging, while still others were chained and put in prison. They were stoned; they were sawed in two; they were put to death by the sword. They went about in sheepskins and goatskins, destitute, persecuted and mistreated—the world was not worthy of them" (my edits).

It's safe to say that there was a pattern in Jerusalem of killing prophets. The Old Testament says so, and the New Testament agrees.

Religious Violence Today

John 3:19-20: "This is the verdict: Light has come into the world, but men loved darkness instead of light because their deeds were evil. Everyone who does evil hates the light, and will not come into the light for fear that his deeds will be exposed."

Ask an average "good, church-going" person to read this passage in John and then ask for illustrations of deeds that are evil. In many cases a layman's definitions of evil will be correct, but in most cases, they will be far from complete. For example, according to Jesus, the evil that thrives within the dark and musty corridors of institutionalized religion actually hates the Light of the world.

Religion at large attempts to run away from the spotlight Jesus trained on religious hatred and cruelty. Christ-less religion might say that the seven woes Jesus directed at religion in Matthew 23 were addressed specifically to the Judean professional religionists. It is true that he specifically identified them and their ancestors' pattern of cruelty and violence toward God's true prophets.

But religious violence is recognizable in all times and all places in human history. Religious violence is an inevitable product of Christ-less, fundamentalist, legalistic religion, followed to its most logical and extreme conclusion.

When religion meets God's grace, religion goes ballistic. When religious traditions, rituals, ceremonies and cherished beliefs are threatened, people kill each other as what they believe to be "a service to God." In reality, when religious people kill in the name of God they are serving their religious taskmasters who enslave them.

Religion enslaves—Jesus liberates. Religion condemns —Jesus pardons. Religion produces pain, heartache and tears—Jesus heals and wipes away the tears. Religion records and remembers, heaping on shame and guilt—Jesus forgives. Religion teaches and insists upon its cherished, unique truth-claims—Jesus is the truth.

Legalistic, oppressive Christ-less religions fly the flag of Christ, but are no more part of him than those who do not even claim to be followers of Jesus. We must not forget the attempts by Christendom to "evangelize" people all around the world whom it deemed to be pagans (and other pejorative terms).

Recent history includes several "Christian" empires that attempted to violently colonize not-so-advanced areas of the world in the name of God—places like Africa, India, Asia, North, Central and South America.

Just a few centuries ago Christendom felt justified in bringing people into what it called "the kingdom of God" at any price—by the sword, torture, intimidation and brutality. While such methodologies are distinctly frowned on in North America and Europe today, intimidation and threats, in the name of God, continue. Many of the practices of religious "evangelism" are justified by a maxim religion otherwise deplores—the end justifies the means.

Lest I appear to be too hard on Christ-less religion that thrives within Christendom (is it possible to be "too hard" on such perversions of the gospel?) let's briefly consider the obvious (to North Americans and Europeans at least) examples of religion gone wild within the world of Islam. After all, it's far easier for a Christian culture to see the flaws of another religion, and in so doing perhaps see a variation of that flaw within its own beliefs and practices.

Honor killings are the practice of a family and/or religious community where someone is killed for doing something that dishonors the name of their family, community or religion. Most honor killings result from infractions involving religiously prohibited sexual behaviors. The killings are justified as an act of face-saving purification of the honored name of the family or religious community.

The United Nations Population Fund estimates that the annual worldwide total of honor-killing victims may be as high as 5,000—an average of almost 14 a day! Most of these are women in Muslim cultures. Honor killings are an example of the most extreme expression of religious violence— here are *five steps or stages leading to religious violence:*

Stage One—Acceptance: Acceptance of the belief that rules, regulations and rituals build a relationship with God is the first stage which actually lays the groundwork for religious violence. Within Christendom, Christ-less religion is the belief that our performance of prescribed rules and rituals is the only way to please or appease God, and that our standing with God is dependent upon the quality of our performance. The idea that what we do enhances or improves our standing with God, so that he will love us more because of our performance (more than he would have had we not put forth the effort) is the un-grace of religion. This "philosophy" by definition involves no grace, no relationship, and therefore no Jesus. This "philosophy" is religion—rules and performance. Performance-based religion itself is the foundation which can lead to violence and bloodshed.

Stage Two—Immersion: After buying into the belief that performance of rituals and rules determines a loving relationship with God, many become even more deeply involved in religion. They immerse themselves in a religious organization/charismatic teacher whereby their religious progress can be monitored and directed. Within this religious cocoon and holy huddle they can be guided by professional religionists and co-religionists who preach and preside over a philosophy of self-salvation by works. Those who practice Stage Two religion are deluded into thinking that God is happy with them because they are doing what the religious organization prescribes. This stage often blurs the distinction between God and human religious authorities.

Stage Three—Indoctrination: Those who descend to Stage Three become true believers. Without reservation those who are enslaved to religion embrace rules of measurement whereby they condemn not only themselves, but everyone else—within their own religious institution and without. Followers of religion who function at Stage Three are fully indoctrinated, becoming religious addicts. Those unfortunates who are imprisoned in this stage begin to accept their religious organization and its religious authorities as "the word of God" and "his only true, anointed prophets/leaders" on earth.

Stage Four—Extremism: Religious slaves who experience Stage Four find themselves in some of the deepest cesspools and most foul swamps religion has to offer. Extremism begins to characterize those who are hopelessly in bondage to their particular religious chain gang. In some cases, individuals at this stage blow up abortion clinics while others blow up civilian targets of the "Great Satan." Those in Stage Four have so totally bought into religion that they have sold their soul to the devil. Once individuals believe they are acting on behalf of God, physical violence often follows. This violence in the name of God can be turned inward, as in self-inflicted wounds, self-flagellation, self-starvation, and the like. It can be aimed at fellow religious organizational members as punishment for infractions in the form of beatings, isolation, exposure, and even torture. When the violence is directed toward one's own peers, then it is thought to be "for their own good." Of course, the violence also targets perceived enemies of God on the outside using vandalism, muggings, torture and the severing of body parts. Rules must be obeyed to please God. Punishing rule-breakers pleases God. Stage Four stops short of murder, which leads us to Stage Five.

Stage Five—Fanaticism: The most toxic and danger-ous religious slaves are somewhat like robots, so brainwashed that they will take human life in the name of God. Enemies on religious hit lists may be inside or outside of the organization. Lynchings, honor killings, assassinations, public beheadings and suicide bombings are all too familiar examples of reli-giously-motivated killings. Religious fanatics who experience Stage Five become judges and executioners, and if "martyred" they become a hero to their fellow-extremists. In Stage Five, all pain is projected outward, and the enemy is identified, hat-ed, attacked and annihilated. All inner ugliness is projected onto "sinners"—all hate (especially self loathing) is project-ed onto "heretics," all of whom must die.

Al Qaeda, by all reports, is a Stage Five religious organ-ization. The Judean leaders of the 1st century A.D. were perhaps a Stage Three organization with some Stage Four elements, and with an unfortunate pattern of using some of its followers who "progressed" into Stage Five when deemed necessary. They were no Al Qaeda. But they were no sewing circle either.

The common denominator, the common ingredient pres-ent in all five stages is the rejection of God's grace. Each stage progressively diminishes critical freedom and thought, and becomes more legalistically demanding than the one before. It all begins with the religious delusion to which humans so easily fall for—the glorification of human per-formance. All this hatred, bigotry, violence and mayhem begins with religion.

The Holocaust: Can It Be Forgiven?

As a young boy I read one of the earliest versions of *Anne Frank—The Diary of a Young Girl*, and I struggled to rec-oncile a loving God with the unimaginable evil of the Holocaust. It was the first time I doubted the existence of God. More than half a century later, I still wrestle with the implications of the Holocaust—the carefully orchestrated, systematic persecution, torture and mass murder of some six million Jews by Nazi Germany.

Under Adolph Hitler, the Nazis proclaimed the Jews to be genetically inferior and a threat to the purity of the Aryan race. The Nazis also included other groups in their mass extermination campaign, often called the "Final Solution." Gypsies, Poles, Russians, Communists, Socialists, homosexuals, religious dissidents such as the Jehovah's Witnesses, mentally and physically disabled Germans, as well as all "enemies" of the state who did not support the Nazi hate campaign were also targeted.

The Holocaust is one of the great historical lessons of what happens when pernicious, toxic and evil ideas are not challenged. All ideas have consequences, and there is no doubt that religious ideas have real and tragic consequences. The rapacious demands of institutionalized religion hold one of the sordid secrets behind the Holocaust.

Can the atrocities of the Holocaust be forgiven? And, beyond the wretched, vicious and monstrous evils of the Holocaust, can self-serving religion that exploits, molests and violates human bodies and souls in the name of God, be forgiven?

Anyone familiar with basic history will remember the Catholic Inquisitions, when torture was used to extract an acceptance of "Jesus Christ" so that the soul whose body was being tortured would be assured of an eternity with God in heaven (rather than an eternity of torture in hell). It made perfect sense at the time. A little torture now will save an eternity of torture later.

Two toxic, religious presuppositions fanned the flames of the torture inflicted by the perpetrators of the Inquisition: 1) God had given an exclusive franchise here on earth to the Roman Catholic church, so that they and they alone had the sole right to represent him. 2) Anyone who died before becoming a Catholic would burn in hell, forever and ever—subjected to eternal torture.

Both of these fatally flawed religious assumptions are alive and well today, and they continue to lead to untold bloodshed. History teaches us that religious zealots who conscientiously perform religious behaviors eventually use extreme measures against those who either disagree with them or are not diligent enough. It was, of course, religious attitudes, assumptions, beliefs and practices that caused so-called moral, good religious people to crucify Jesus, God in the flesh.

Bonhoeffer and Ten Boom—
Forgiveness Out of the Ashes

One of Hitler's greatest victories was his triumph over the soul of Christianity in Germany—the majority of those who called themselves Christians capitulated to his demands. While not everyone agreed with each decision that increasingly dehumanized Jews, the majority of German Christians, including judges, professors, priests and pastors went along with Hitler's hate-filled agenda.

Dietrich Bonhoeffer and Corrie Ten Boom were exceptions. Bonhoeffer, a pastor, resisted the Nazis from the beginning, believing that Christ alone was the king, and that no government could exercise ultimate spiritual control over Christians. The Nazis responded by forbidding Bohhoeffer to preach or teach (much like anti-Semite Mahmoud Ahmadinejad does with anyone who resists him in today's Iran).

Bonhoeffer became a part of the German resistance and was eventually involved in one of the plots to kill Hitler. Bonhoeffer also helped Jews flee from the Nazi death machine, and for that reason he was arrested and imprisoned. He was eventually executed—only a few weeks before Hitler committed suicide.

Since his death, Dietrich Bonhoeffer has grown to be a legendary pioneer among contemporary voices calling for the reformation of Christianity. His term "religion-less Christianity" has inspired me, as I see the need to move Christians away from unquestioned obedience to institutionalized rules and regulations so that they may be truly free in Christ. Bonhoeffer believed that he must resist Hitler's evils—as a Christ-follower he could see no other alternative.

Because she helped harbor Jews from the Nazis, Corrie Ten Boom, born in Holland (1892), was eventually taken to Ravensbruck concentration camp in Germany. Corrie Ten Boom survived her brutal experience, and after Ravensbruck was liberated, she lived the rest of her life writing and speaking about the forgiveness we may have in and through Jesus Christ.

When the Nazis invaded Holland (the Netherlands) in 1940, Corrie and her family became active in the Dutch underground, helping to rescue many Jews from death at the hands of the Nazi SS. Many Jews survived because of a hiding place that had been built into a wardrobe in Corrie's bedroom (hence the name of her well-known book, *The Hiding Place*).

With the help of a Dutch informant the Germans arrested the Ten Boom family on February 28, 1944. Corrie's father died in prison, and her sister Betsie died while she and Corrie were held in Ravensbruck.

After her release at the end of the war, Corrie returned to Holland to help other concentration camp survivors. Before her death in 1983 she traveled the world for speaking engagements, discussing God's love and forgiveness, and authored a number of books.

In her book, *Tramp for the Lord*, Corrie tells the story of how she came face to face with one of the most cruel Ravensbruck camp guards. It was 1947, only three years after this man participated in the brutalities that, among other things, took her sister Betsie's life.

"It was in a church in Munich that I first saw him—a balding, heavy-set man in a gray overcoat, a brown felt hat clutched between

his hands. People were filing out of the basement room where I had just spoken...

And that's when I saw him, working his way forward against the others. One moment I saw the overcoat and the brown hat; the next, a blue uniform and a visored cap with its skull and cross-bones. It came back with a rush: the huge room with its harsh over-head lights; and pathetic pile of dresses and shoes in the center of the floor; the shame of walking naked past this man.

The place was Ravensbruck and the man who was making his way forward had been a guard—one of the most cruel guards. Now he was in front of me, hand thrust out: 'A fine message, Fraulein. How good it is to know that, as you say, all our sins are at the bot-tom of the sea!'

And I, who had spoken so glibly of forgiveness, fumbled in my pock-etbook rather than take that hand. He would not remember me, of course—how could he remember one prisoner among those thousands of women?

But I remembered him and the leather crop swinging from his belt. I was face to face with one of my captors and my blood seemed to freeze...It could have been many seconds that he stood there—hand held out – but to me it seemed hours as I wrestled with the most difficult thing I had ever had to do...

And still I stood there with the coldness clutching my heart. Jesus help me! I prayed silently....

And so woodenly, mechanically, I thrust my hand into the one stretched out to me. As I did, an incredible thing took place. The cur-rent started in my shoulder, raced down my arms, sprang into our joined hands. And then this healing warmth seemed to flood my whole being, bringing tears to my eyes.

'I forgive you, brother!' I cried. 'With all my heart.' I had nev-er known God's love so intensely as I did then. But even so, I real-ized it was not my love. I had tried, and I did not have the pow-er...." (Tramp for the Lord, Corrie Ten Boom, pp. 57-59).

Forgiveness—God's Answer to Religious Violence

Corrie Ten Boom illustrates the forgiveness which is a gift of God's amazing grace—the forgiveness which is made so confusing by the Christ-less religion which thrives within much of Christendom. Christ-less religion believes that God will only forgive us as and when we forgive others, and cites Jesus' teaching in Matthew 6:12 as proof:

Matthew 6:12: "Forgive our debts, as we also have forgiven our debtors."

Those who accept and believe a Christ-less interpretation of this passage unwittingly turn God's forgiveness into a conditional act, which depends on human merit. But if God forgives us only as and when we forgive others, then his forgiveness depends on an action we must first take, and which, in turn, gives us the power to earn God's forgiveness.

What Jesus is saying in Matthew 6:12 is that God makes it possible for us to forgive others. The only true, lasting and eternal forgiveness a human may offer another human is a gift which only God can give. Apart from God, humans are incapable of offering divine forgiveness to one another. Just as Corrie Ten Boom found it impossible to humanly forgive her former tormentor, so too are we incapable of mustering true forgiveness from some depth of our soul.

We are able to forgive others because God does not wait to see if we will forgive others before he forgives us. If his forgiveness were conditional upon our perfect forgiveness of others, then no human would ever be forgiven. His forgiveness is conditioned and based on his goodness, not our own. His forgiveness is given to us by his grace, not because of any action or behavior we can humanly produce.

Romans 5:8: "But God demonstrates his own love for us in this: While we were still sinners, Christ died for us."

While suffering his excruciating death on the cross, Jesus prayed:

Luke 23:34: "Father, forgive them, for they do not know what they are doing."

But surely those who beat and tortured him, those who nailed him to the cross, and those who insulted and cursed him as he hung dying, knew what they were doing? What did Jesus mean?

I believe that Jesus was saying that they had no idea that they were actually taking the life of God the Son, God in the flesh, their own Creator, the second Person of the tri-une Godhead. Jesus knew that many humans had some direct responsibility for killing him. Yet Jesus was clearly stating that God's forgiveness does not depend on human abilities. God's forgiveness is unconditional—no matter how much culpability you or I may have.

That's why you and I cannot give divine forgiveness to another human, apart from God's grace. We cannot give what we do not possess. We cannot participate in God's forgiveness unless we have first accepted his grace, which itself entails an acceptance and even a surrender on our part—a realization that we do not have what it takes to forgive others, or for that matter, ourselves.

God's limitless love means that his forgiveness is inclusive, rather than exclusive. It's not just for people who have all their doctrinal ducks lined up, or who memorize the right creed, say the right prayer or sing the right tune. God's forgiveness breaks the chain of an eye for an eye, by transforming our pain. If our pain is not transformed by God's grace, then we will transmit that pain. We will, apart from God's grace, be consumed by the pain of what we have suffered, and it will be manifested as hatred and vengeance.

The Holocaust will always stand as a brutal example of the extremes of human inhumanity toward other humans. The Holocaust teaches us that nothing—no human remedy (no religion, no rituals no penance, no human atonement) is enough to bring us to God. Only God can do that. Only God can give us forgiveness. It takes God to forgive the evils of the Holocaust—and he has. It happened on the cross of Christ.

Our Prayer:

Lord, deceived by Christ-less religion, some of us have spiritually abused others, while the vast majority of us have been victims of such abuse. Because we have often acted like snakes, we ask forgiveness, not simply for our sins, but for the religious practices we have blindly followed and obeyed, thinking we were serving you. Forgive us, we pray.

Chapter 9

A Never Ending River of Living Water

"O Jerusalem, Jerusalem, you who kill the prophets and stone those sent to you, how often I have longed to gather your children together, as a hen gathers her chicks under her wings, but you were not willing. Look, your house is left to you desolate. For I tell you, you will not see me again until you say, 'Blessed is he who comes in the name of the Lord'"—Matthew 23:37-39

Extreme Makeover: Home Edition is a reality television series providing much needed home remodels and renovations for families who have no resources of their own for such an undertaking. Each episode features a family in the middle of a crisis, whose life is in shambles. Sometimes the family is facing a terminal illness, and at other times the family is living in a dilapidated home, heavily damaged from a natural disaster. While the family is sent on a vacation, the producers work with construction crews to renovate, remodel and sometimes, in cases where the home is beyond repair, completely replace their home.

Religion has so damaged our lives and our spiritual homes that we are all in desperate need of an *Extreme Makeover*. While the television series can only provide physical makeovers for a few families, God offers extreme spiritual makeovers for each one of us. Like the television series, God does for us what we cannot do for ourselves. He pays the bill that neither we nor anyone else can afford to pay.

The **seven woes** of Matthew 23 are a description of the hurricane-like destruction that religion leaves in its wake. As this sermon concludes, Jesus offers a solution to the desolation he has described. Jesus explains his desire to give each and every human being a total spiritual transformation. He's not offering a new coat of paint or a few minor repairs. He is offering a new spiritual home, a new life— not simply a patched up version of the religious disaster we have experienced thus far. We are in the mess we are in because of the shifting sands of religion (Matthew 7:24-27), so he offers us a new foundation for our faith, the firm foundation he alone can provide.

After exposing the disaster and catastrophe caused by religion in his **seven woes**, after an unremitting castigation of religion and all its legalisms, Jesus comes back to the foundation of his teaching. He offers love. He offers love to this group of hypocrites, liars, snakes and murderers. As an illustration of his love, Jesus uses one of the most beautiful poetic images of God's protective care in Scripture—a hen's care for her chicks. How could he offer protective care for this group of scoundrels and miscreants?

It's hard for us to see Jesus offering love after his powerful judgment against religion and its authorities. But Jesus did. Why? Everything God says and does springs out of love —for love is his fundamental, core essence. God's love desires to liberate people from death-dealing religion. God's love aches to clean up spiritual refugees who have washed up on the shore, coated with oil-slick-like globs of toxic, religious tar. God's love and grace yearns to give all humans a new life—a second life—a spiritual rebirth. God's love and grace profoundly desires to deliver us all from spiritual captivity. In the name of his love for them, Jesus blasted the religion that caused these religious leaders to become legalistic fanatics. Jesus held up a mirror to their false faces to show them what religion had turned them into: spiritually dead religionists whose toxic legalism was contagious and hazardous to the spiritual health of those they served.

This is the final saying from Jesus in Matthew 23, at face value another stinging diatribe against religion, but upon closer examination, evidence that Jesus is offering the cleansing fire of God's grace and love to those whom he loves. The following five facts about his closing words in his final sermon on earth demonstrate that he loves even venomous, toxic spiritual snakes.

Fact One: Jesus Laments Jerusalem —Held Captive by Religion

Jesus begins the signature passage for this chapter with the phrase, "O Jerusalem, Jerusalem." These words echo the Old Testament prophets, Jeremiah in particular, who also used the phrase, "O Jerusalem" (Jeremiah 4:14, 6:8, 13:27, 15:5). Jesus uses the language of Old Testament prophets to bravely chastise a city known for killing such prophets. "O Jerusalem, Jerusalem," is an emotional vehicle loaded with emotional cargo, a phrase heavy with passion.

Neither our passage in Matthew 23:37-39 nor Luke's version of the same statement (Luke 13:34-35) describe Jesus as weeping over Jerusalem. Luke specifically records another occasion when he wept over Jerusalem, when he entered the city on a donkey, on what we today call Palm Sunday (Luke 19:29-49). In that story, Jesus weeps and prophesies against the city as he arrives at the temple. Then he gets off the donkey, enters the temple, and drives out those who are engaging in commercial activities. Popularly called "The Cleansing of the Temple" this event is recorded in all four Gospels. While there is no mention of his weeping over Jerusalem during his Matthew 23 sermon, tears would have been appropriate, and he may well have shed a few on that occasion.

"O Jerusalem, Jerusalem" is a lament, in part, because the phrase repeats the word "Jerusalem." To say "O Jerusalem" is a prophetic cry of lament, for sure. But to say "O Jerusalem, Jerusalem" is to double the intensity.

Jerusalem and all that it stood for was giving Jesus a double dose of pain. After saying "O Jerusalem, Jerusalem" Jesus repeats what we verified and discussed in the previous chapter of this book: The city and the religion it represents has a history of killing messengers from God.

Matthew 23:37: "O Jerusalem, Jerusalem, you who kill the prophets and stone those sent to you...."

God keeps sending prophets to this city because he loves it, but his messengers are consistently met with rejection, abuse and murder. Jesus' pain is undoubtedly intensified by his own personal mission, to go to Jerusalem, and his foreknowledge that he, too, will be rejected and killed there.

Why does Jesus' rejection, inspired by religion, hurt him so profoundly? The simple answer is love. In the face of their lethal response to God and his messengers, Jesus, God in the flesh, still has a heart full of love for Jerusalem, including its professional religionists who embody and direct so much of the religious abuse. Jesus embodies the love of God.

Fact Two: Jesus Longs to Love the Religious Leaders in Jerusalem

Jesus reveals the unfathomable love and immeasurable grace of God with these tender words: "How often I have longed to gather your children together, as a hen gathers her chicks under her wings..." Incredible! Without hesitation or qualification Jesus openly expresses that he *longs* for those who opposed, persecuted and eventually would torture and crucify him. Oh how he *longed* for them! The biblical Greek word for longing is *thelo*. Among other things, *thelo* means:

to will, have in mind, intend; to be resolved or determined, to purpose; to desire, to wish; to love; to like to do a thing, be fond of doing; to take delight in...

What love is this! Jesus loves this city, ironically called the city of peace, which epitomizes the core and center of oppressive, legalistic religion. Jesus is determined to be in relationship with all those addicted to religion—he burns with the white hot fire of God's love for them. He aches to remove all of the oily, toxic residue of religion from their hearts and souls. He is affectionate and fond of them, in spite of their religiously-driven animosity for him. Jesus takes sheer pleasure in loving them. Jesus longs for them. Nothing can change or diminish God's love for us!

Earlier in his ministry Jesus illustrated the cleansing, life giving effect of his ministry, based on God's grace and love:

John 7:37-38: "If anyone is thirsty, let him come to me and drink. Whoever believes in me, as the Scripture has said, streams of living water will flow from within him."

Water imparts life, as well as being an agent of cleansing. In the last chapter of the book of Revelation, Jesus inspires John to describe a healing, cleansing, life-giving river which flows through the new Jerusalem. In breath-taking symbolism, Jesus reveals the heavenly city of Jerusalem, the picture of the kingdom of heaven, in stark contrast to the Jerusalem (and its religious system) which crucified him:

Revelation 22:1-2: "Then the angel showed me the river of the water of life, as clear as crystal, flowing from the throne of God and of the Lamb down the middle of the great street of the city."

The love of God is truly a never ending river. Within this same book of Revelation, Jesus described his rejection by religion. As the Gospel of John says, he was rejected by "his own" (John 1:11). We often read that passage within its historical context, thinking that John had reference to a time long, long ago—almost 2,000 years ago—in a land far, far away—the real estate we today know as the Holy Land. We often think that John's reference is primarily about the Jews, a racial and religious people who are far, far away from our Christian faith. But in the book of Revelation Jesus explains that he is rejected by his own church! The church in Laodicea, his own church, had kicked him out and did not realize what they had done. Still, Jesus stands at the door knocking:

Revelation 3:19: *"Those whom I love I rebuke and discipline."*

The One who rebukes Jerusalem loves Jerusalem with a passion. What more profound picture can you imagine than the one Jesus gives? Jesus likens himself to a mother hen. Amazing! Think about it.

The God-character in the parabolic imagery Jesus used to depict his undying love is a mother chicken. After a hen's chicks hatch, she guards them with her life by brooding them together underneath her wings. It is interesting that brooding in English today means moodily dwelling on something. But when a hen broods, she is single-mindedly devoted to one thing: *keeping her chicks safe and warm by defending them with her own body.*

Jesus was willing to defend Jerusalem with his body too. He was ready to gather in his chicks for gentle warmth and protection. The intimacy and tenderness of this image is almost shocking. What hen could possibly yearn to love and defend these Jerusalem chicks? What a stark contrast Jesus reveals! These chicks are blind fools, snakes and murderers, who rejected the Hen, yet she still loves, she still reaches with her wings, she still fights for their lives—willing to lay down her own for theirs. The cross is Jesus' brooding love.

John 10:11: *"I am the good shepherd. The good shepherd lays down his life for the sheep."*
John 10:18: *"No one takes it* [my life] *from me, but I lay it down of my own accord"* (my edits).

You might say that the main purpose of Jesus becoming one of us was to tell us, and demonstrate to and for us, that God is not at all like what we have been told. Jesus revealed the Father in his teaching and in his behavior. He revealed the Father's love by laying down his own life for us, the sheep of his pasture.

Not only have we misunderstood God the Father, but with a huge assist from Christ-less religion, we have come to misconstrue Jesus, God the Son. Consider the title Christendom has given perhaps the most well known of all of Jesus' parables—the Prodigal Son. The parable is about a prodigal (an old English word meaning recklessly extravagant, lavish, to the point of seeming to be wasteful)—but is the prodigal only the son, or is the father also prodigal?

We have heard much of the wasteful, ungrateful son, who "squandered his wealth" (Luke 15:13). There is no doubt that the son was prodigal. But we don't hear much about the prodigal father of his parable. When the son "came to his senses" (Luke 15:17) he "went to his father" (Luke 15:20). At this point we often are directed to consider the amazing forgiveness of the father.

But the grace of the father is not only exemplified by his forgiveness, his amazing grace is also prodigal! He is recklessly extravagant, lavish and seemingly wasteful. To the astonishment of everyone, including his son, the father accepts his son back without reservation. There is no probation for his son. There is only unabashed joy, which morphs into a celebration. The older brother, who is extremely religious, oh-so careful to do all the right things, is not amused by the extravagant love of his prodigal father, a love which is absolutely undeserved by the younger son. The older brother is scandalized by the gracious, unconditional love of the father.

The older brother of the parable is held captive by the same religious mindset as were the authorities whom Jesus denounces in Matthew 23. Obsessed with bringing about the kingdom of religion, the teachers of the law and the Pharisees failed to realize that the kingdom of heaven was among them (Luke 17:21) in the person of Jesus. The kingdom of God's love, available by grace, in and through Jesus Christ, was present with them then and there, and it still is here right now!

Revelation 3:20: "Here I am! I stand at the door and knock."

149

Jesus has the same patient longing that he felt even for his enemies in Jerusalem for all of us—Jew, Muslim, Hindu, agnostic, atheist—even some of the really obnoxious Christians we all know. He loves to long for us. His love is a never-ending river. Oh how he longs for us all, wishing to gather us under his wings like a mother hen tenderly protects her chicks with her own warm body! And when we shut him out, he patiently knocks and longs for us to open again to him. Jesus offers his love to even the hardest of hearts, hearts that have become resistant and somewhat immune to God's grace by the relentless propaganda of death-dealing religion.

The other side of Jesus' longing to bring each of us under his wings is his desire to bring us under his wings *together*. The invitation is not merely for an individual relationship with him. We are his brood of chicks together, brought together as brothers and sisters, a family in his safekeeping.

The temple was made for people, not the people for the temple. It was so easy to forget this. The Jerusalem religionists served the temple slavishly, arguing about the temple and its procedures. The house of the Lord was meant to bring them together into the warmth of community, but the temple had become a vehicle they used to tear one another apart. Instead of the temple serving to unite them under God's care, it became an idol that enslaved them in religious regulations and rivalry.

The laws of Moses were given to the people for the people, for their relationships, for community, but how quickly the people became slaves of the laws, and their enslavement drove them apart.

Is it not like this in many churches today? The church buildings were made for people, not people for the buildings. Yet churches devolve into **ABC** organizations where people become slaves of statistics, bricks and mortar.

Communion (the Lord's Supper)—a meal designed to bring us together under the wings of heaven has degenerated into factional arguments over leavened or unleavened bread or wafers, juice or wine, chalice or individual cups, kneeling or standing, drinking or dipping, once a year, once a month or once a day, elements understood as symbolic or literal, open to all or reserved for members only.

Religion has perverted the divine meal of fellowship and unity, provided for us in and by the body and blood of Jesus, to drive us apart in factional bickering. We were not made for the meal. The meal was made for us. We are not the hosts. We are the invited guests. How easily we reject true communion with one another in the name of right ritual procedure.

As I understand it, bi-polar disorder is an insidious disease. Those who are bi-polar find it difficult staying on their meds because the disease gives them a false reality, assuring them that everyone else is sick, not them. The result is horrible isolation, which many bipolar sufferers accept because the disease shows them no alternative.

They become paranoid and regard those who are trying to reach out to them as crazy and out to get them. So they run from light and community, choosing an isolated existence with only their cold, dark, lying disease for company. How is the virus of religious legalism any different?

Some argue about communion procedures and details, and who should be allowed to receive communion. Some fight about traditional or contemporary music. Others squabble about which translation of the Bible should be used. Some feel superior because of how much water was used in their baptism and how physically mature they were when they were dunked. We fight over theo-logy and miss *Theos*—God. We congratulate ourselves on "our" truth, about how exalted and great our doctrines and creeds are, and we forget the One and Only. Religion replaces Jesus. Religion rejects Jesus.

How it must grieve Jesus yet today that his brood would rather freeze to death, alone in the dark, than to rest around him, in mutual warmth.

Fact Three: Religious Leaders Reject Jesus' Overtures of Love

*Matthew 23:37: "...how often I have longed to gather your children together, as a hen gathers her chicks under her wings, **but you were not willing**"* (emphasis mine).

Jesus extended his invitation again and again. Jesus reveals that he was not only pained by his unrequited love, he clearly communicated to the scribes and the Pharisees that he knew that they had already said a final *No*—that this final sermon would not make any difference—that they would kill him no matter what he might say.

Jesus challenged what the religious leaders did and taught. He regularly, and publicly, challenged their authority and threatened their power. The Jerusalem authorities perceived him to be a lawbreaker who perverted and undermined their traditions and customs, a dangerous rebel rouser who opposed their religion. Only his death, they believed, would preserve the nation and its uneasy peace with Rome.

As he concludes this sermon, reaching out to those who had rejected him, Jesus recognizes their final *No* to him and therefore to God. What he says next confirms this.

Fact Four: God Has Left the Building

No matter how gilded and ornate, how breathtaking and magnificent a religious edifice might be, when God is rejected God leaves the religious house.

Matthew 23:38: "Look, your house is left to you desolate."

Perhaps Jesus is saying that God had already vacated the holy places of the religion of his day, because they had long ago rejected him. Perhaps Jesus was saying that to whatever degree God still might be "present" in the Jerusalem temple, he would move out once and for all when religion killed Jesus, God the Son, God in the flesh. Perhaps Jesus was pointing to the physical destruction of the Jerusalem temple in 70 A.D. as the beyond-any-doubt sign that God didn't live there anymore.

Mark 13:1: "As he was leaving the temple, one of his disciples said to him, 'Look, Teacher! What massive stones! What magnificent buildings!' 'Do you see all these great buildings?' replied Jesus. 'Not one stone here will be left on another; every one will be thrown down.'"

The house of God was literally laid waste by Rome. It was completely dismantled and burned. All that is left today are the lower retaining walls of the outer temple compound.

There may be more, however, to what Jesus is saying. I wonder if there is a double meaning in Jesus' bleak pronouncement of a God-deserted house of worship. Jesus once argued with the Jerusalem authorities using the word temple in a double way.

*John 2:16-21: "To those who sold doves he said, 'Get these out of here! How dare you turn my Father's house into a market!' His disciples remembered that it is written: 'Zeal for your **house** will consume me.' Then the Jews demanded of him, 'What miraculous sign can you show us to prove your authority to do all this?' Jesus answered them, 'Destroy this **temple**, and I will raise it again in three days.' The Jews replied, 'It has taken forty-six years to build this temple, and you are going to raise it in three days?' But the temple he had spoken of was **his body**"* (emphasis mine).

So when Jesus said, "Look, your house is left to you desolate," perhaps by house he meant both the temple in Jerusalem and the temple of his body. Perhaps this second meaning of Matthew 23:38 is a reference to his own death— that the religious professionals were about to be responsible for making the temple of God, Jesus' own body, desolate and deserted.

Jesus' presence was the physical presence of God in

the flesh. And since the scribes and Pharisees were about to orchestrate his execution, then in a literal sense they were removing God from the Jerusalem temple. They said a seemingly final *No* to his offer of love, and then they had him killed. Thus they were driving God out of his own house.

It was only a few days after this final sermon of Jesus here in Matthew 23 that the Jerusalem authorities, as the driving force behind his torture and execution, ensured that the temple in Jerusalem was well and truly deserted by God. They may not have realized it, but they were killing the very God that they appeared to serve as religious professionals in the temple. That house was indeed made desolate by their own hands.

A similar thing effectively happens within churches throughout Christendom today. Denominations and congregations drive Jesus out. Of course, no religious authority has the power to control the Lord. None of us can *make* him do anything or *stop* him from doing anything. We "drive Jesus out" in the same way that Jesus himself said that the church at Laodicea (Revelation 3: 20) had left him on the outside looking in.

By Jesus' own testimony, the church in Laodicea had, metaphorically speaking, put Jesus outside of the church door and shut it. They had closed their hearts to him. Laodicea drove Jesus out because they felt they didn't need him —they were satisfied with their own religious efforts, they felt that what they were doing was sufficient to ensure God's blessing. Jesus does not force himself on anyone. If you push him out and shut the door, he does not kick it in. He honors your decision.

Churches within Christendom find themselves replicating this situation. They can become impressed with themselves and enamored of their own successes. Churches can become so busy with their programs and outreaches that they forget God's grace.

In many spiritual addresses within North American Christendom today, especially within mega-churches and their many "wannabes," a non-stop buzz of activity promises something for everyone. When the congregation meets in the sanctuary they are enthralled and entertained, even mesmerized by the bells and whistles, the music, the sound, the teaching—it's all attention arresting. Everyone is so engrossed in what they are "doing" that no one seems to hear the persistent knocking at the door.

When we, individually or corporately, possess and maintain all of the physical and spiritual achievements and stuff we think we need, we normally credit ourselves and our programs and our obedience and our effort and therefore deny our own spiritual neediness. We can so easily perceive ourselves as independent of and from God, rather than dependent on him.

We can have confidence in our abilities (and those of our church and its doctrines, teachings, creeds, rituals and ceremonies)—we can take pride in spiritual accomplishments, and those of our church—we can be comforted by the traditions and heritage of our church—and "not realize that you are wretched, pitiful, poor, blind and naked" (Revelation 3:7). The Lord paints a picture of himself—knocking on the door of those who are comfortable and self-satisfied.

There is a further meaning we can glean from Jesus' declaration, "Look, your house is left to you desolate," in what he says next.

Fact Five: Jesus Is the One Who Comes in the Name of the Lord

In the play *Green Pastures*, the angel Gabriel is depicted as approaching God while God is deep in thought. God is concerned that people on earth do not seem to be listening to the Old Testament prophets and messengers he sends. Gabriel becomes angry and offers to blow the trumpet at once, ending human history as we know it. But God takes the trumpet away from Gabriel.

Gabriel protests that humans never listen to the messengers God sends. God responds, "I am not going to send anybody this time. I am going myself." Some have called the coming of God in the person of Jesus the "great exchange." The great exchange was truly "such a deal." In return for our rejection of God, in return for the crucifixion, to which God knew religion would subject him to, Jesus came with peace and love. The peace and love is still the basis of the relationship he offers to the entire world—in spite of our behavior, certainly not because of it!

Jesus closed his sermon with this prediction and promise: "For I tell you, you will not see me again until you say, 'Blessed is he who comes in the name of the Lord.'" (Matthew 23:39) He was quoting Psalm 118:26. And with this prediction and promise he ends his final sermon:

Psalm 118:26: "Blessed is he who comes in the name of the LORD. From the house of the LORD we bless you."

As he concludes this sermon in Matthew 23, the chorus of the crowds who had welcomed him in what we often refer to as his triumphal entry into the city of Jerusalem were still ringing in his ears. Those crowds sang the words of Psalm 118:26, "Blessed is he who comes in the name of the Lord" (Matthew 21:9). The worship and adulation given to Jesus by the crowds on what we now know as Palm Sunday were no doubt ringing in the ears of the religious leaders as well—in their case it hardened their resolve to end the threat Jesus posed to the religious status quo.

Of course, though the crowds welcomed Jesus, they did so out of their own desire that he drive out the hated Romans and give them physical peace and prosperity. As he entered Jerusalem for the last time during his earthly ministry, the crowds greeted him as someone they felt would fulfill their agenda. They were not welcoming him as the suffering servant, the Lamb of God who would willingly submit to the humiliation and embarrassment of crucifixion. The people wanted military victory, vindication and economic relief— they were not praising Jesus for bringing them relief from religious enslavement.

Napoleon once returned from battle, greeted by crowds singing his praises. Michel Ney, whom Napoleon called "the bravest of the brave" was with Napoleon as they rode in procession through the cheering throng. Ney turned to Napoleon and said, "Listen! You must find this quite satisfying." Napoleon quickly responded, "Nonsense. With a small change in circumstances these same people would be shouting for me to go to the gallows."

When the masses that welcomed Jesus to Jerusalem realized that he would not give them what they wanted, that "change in circumstances" caused them to drastically change their tune. After all, as we noted earlier, blessing those who come in the name of the Lord is precisely what Jerusalem and its religious authorities had a track record of not doing. Instead of a welcome, they persecuted, mocked, imprisoned and killed servants of the Lord.

It will take nothing less than the Second Coming to completely transform religious dysfunction. The only hope to end holy wars once and for all—the only hope for complete healing of religious corruption and blindness is the return of God the Son whom religion itself crucified.

The love of God shines through this final comment of Jesus' sermon. Jesus doesn't end this sermon with threats and fulmination. Isn't it ironic how fear-based religion which passes for Christianity characterizes the Second Coming of Jesus as a time when he finally gets so upset with all of us that he has to "come down here" and "take us to the woodshed for a good, old-fashioned whoopin"? As he concludes this, his last sermon, Jesus doesn't say "I'll come back and then you'll get yours."

It seems as Jesus concludes this sermon he is saying, "You will see me again, Jerusalem. On that day I will hear all of you say, 'Blessed is the one who comes in the name of the Lord.' Truly I say to you, the great day is coming when it will be self evident that the one you killed is the one you will acknowledge. On the day of the Lord you will see what you have done, and you will see and accept God's forgiveness at the same time. And because of that forgiveness, you will bless the one whom you rejected and killed."

After pronouncing his most severe chastisements, after expressing his most tender longing, and after disclosing his undying love, Jesus closes his sermon with the promise of all promises—*I'll be back.*

Our Prayer:

Lord, we are so good at shooting ourselves in the foot. We drive you out even though deep down inside we know you are our only hope. Just as Jerusalem killed Jesus in the name of preserving the status quo of its religion, we often drive Jesus out of our midst as we keep busy with programs and activities we feel we are doing in your name. We are so blind. Help us to see your longing heart. Thank you for living in us that we might live in you, by your grace. Thank you for inclusively extending the riches of your grace to the entire world, without reservation, forever and ever.

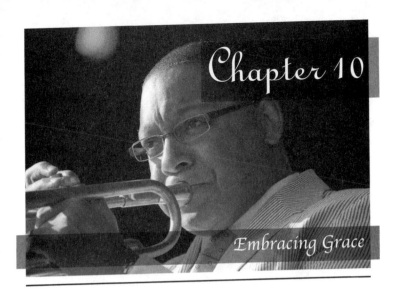

Chapter 10

Embracing Grace

Wynton Marsalis is an internationally acclaimed musician, composer, bandleader and jazz artist. Proclaimed as one of the greatest trumpeters of all time, Marsalis performs and loves classical music in addition to all forms of jazz.

In a Greenwich Village concert, Marsalis was pouring his heart into a performance, reaching the final dramatic notes just as a cell phone in the audience interrupted him with an electronic, singsong melody. As the cell-phone offender ran outside to take the call the glorious moment seemed to be lost. The entire performance seemed ready to unravel as the once silent room, focused solely on the magic of Marsalis' performance, started to fill with the sounds of nervous shuffling of chairs and whispered conversation.

Marsalis paused—his eyebrows arched. Frozen behind the microphone, Marsalis graciously replayed the cell-phone melody note for note. Then he repeated it, and began improvising on the tune. The audience slowly came back to him. In a few minutes he resolved the improvisation—which had changed keys once or twice and throttled down to a ballad tempo—and then he returned to the moment in time when the sour notes of the cell-phone had so rudely interrupted his incomparable music. As he played the last few notes of the ballad the crowd erupted, applauding his improvised grace notes.

Grace as Improvisation

"The church, by and large, has had a poor record of encouraging freedom. It has spent so much time inculcating in us the fear of making mistakes that it has made us like ill-taught piano students: we play our pieces, but we never really hear them because our main concern is not to make music, but to avoid some flub that will get us in Dutch" (*Between Noon and Three*, Robert Farrar Capon, page 149).

God came to us in the person of Jesus, embracing the fact of our sour notes, improvising them and transforming them, by his grace. By virtue of becoming one of us, he condescended to play the silly little tunes of our lives, taking our discord and dissonance and graciously reconciling and reforming it. It couldn't have been any other way.

How could he have fixed the sour notes of our lives without playing our personal tune? How could he transform us with the magic of his melody without acknowledging our discord, gracefully playing back to us our individual ugly little bleeps, and then masterfully improvising on our sour notes, transforming them into his melodious magic? It's called grace—God's grace as improvisation.

God improvises our out-of-sync, discordant notes by his grace, in and through Jesus. Do you remember the old fairy tale where a beautiful princess kisses a frog and in so doing transforms the frog into a handsome prince? When God became one of us, the fairy tale reversed itself. The beautiful princess (Jesus) became a frog like us, so that we could be transformed. God didn't just remain aloof, conducting the orchestra and correcting its mistakes from afar—but he actually stepped off the podium and joined us:

John 1:14: The Word became flesh and blood, and moved into the neighborhood (The Message).

Religion insists that we play what it considers to be the right notes, coloring inside the lines it has drawn. As religion teaches (indoctrinates) us, we become more concerned about not angering God than we are in soaring by his grace. God's grace frees us from the religious gravity that holds us down. My good friend, Monte Wolverton, recalls a time earlier in his life when he was teaching an elementary art class to young children. A father arrived to watch the class in progress, and as he observed his six-year-old daughter, he found himself unable to accept her freedom of expression.

He sat down, and erased all that his daughter had done, and as Monte (the teacher) watched, the father became the teacher of art. The daughter drew a line, the father erased it, and then while holding her hand drew the "correct" line. This process continued until the end of the class. Looking back, Monte wonders what eventually happened to that young girl who could do nothing right in the eyes of her father. Did she wind up as yet another victim of mechanical, unfeeling perfectionism, forever worried about making a mistake?

The crucifixion, the mother of all magic-killing moments, became the high and holy moment of improvisational grace. Jesus took the ugliest tune of all and sang it with all his heart, so that the depraved theme of human violence and hate, sin and death might not be the last note. The cacophony of the crucifixion was sung by the Creator, such that the most strident noise imaginable was transformed into the song of angels:

Revelation 5:12: "*Worthy is the Lamb, who was slain, to receive power and wealth and wisdom and strength and honor and glory and praise!*"

Jesus doesn't condemn our tone-deaf chorus. He joins the choir. And look who he selected for the original choir. Peter, a brassy fishermen whose song always seemed to fall flat, was handpicked by the Lord to tune the orchestra. God transformed the Saul of religion, an insufferable music snob, into a performance artist who gave concerts of grace. Jesus is not looking for people with perfect pitch (just another reason why the gospel really is good news!). What he is looking for is people who will invite him to sing along with them, and yield to his grace improvisations.

Listen to the squawking coming from so many of our churches! The acrimonious bellowing and griping sounds we produce are like the screech of fingernails on a chalkboard to God. Are we so preoccupied with patting our feet to silly little religious melodies that we can't hear the music of the Master? Have we grown so weary of working in religious salt mines that we give no thought to the decidely un-Christlike martial music religion plays for us, as we march along endlessly attempting to please God?

And yet, the Master came to be one of us. Can you hear him? He is even now playing back the empty, soul-destroying religious dirges, improvising on them so that by grace we can become free. With Paul (Romans 8:38) I am convinced that neither squawk nor squeak, neither blare nor bleep, neither sour note nor tone deaf wail, nor any droning organ prelude, neither contemporary praise and worship nor Pentecostal polka, nor any gospel music in all creation, will be able to separate us from the melody of grace that is in Christ Jesus our Lord.

The word reconciliation means to *bring back a former state of harmony*. Reconciliation between you (humanity) and God is a done deal:

Romans 5:10-11: "For if, when we were God's enemies, we were reconciled to him through the death of his Son, how much more, having been reconciled, shall we be saved through his life! Not only is this so, but we also rejoice in God through our Lord Jesus Christ, through whom we have now received reconciliation."
2 Corinthians 5:18-19: "All this is from God, who reconciled us to himself through Christ and gave us the ministry of reconciliation: that God was reconciling the world to himself in Christ, not counting men's sins against them. And he has committed to us the message of reconciliation."
Colossians 1:19-20: "For God was pleased to have all his fullness dwell in him [Jesus], and through him to reconcile to himself

all things, whether things on earth or things in heaven, by making peace through his blood, shed on the cross" (my edits).

When "God showed his love among us" (1 John 4:9) he had no guarantee that we would love him back. He made the first move. He did all that was necessary—"He sent his one and only Son into the world that we might live through him" (1 John 4:9). He has done all that is necessary for us to live in Christ. He stepped into our lives—he made the first move:

John 1:14: "The Word became flesh and blood, and moved into the neighborhood" (The Message).

When I think of God, in Christ, moving into our neighborhood and making the first move, I often remember a story about my all-time favorite president, Abraham Lincoln. When he was campaigning for the presidency, he received a letter from an eight-year old girl. The little girl suggested that Lincoln should grow a beard to hide his rather homely face.

Lincoln wasn't offended—he read the letter and sent a thank-you to the young girl. He told her that if his campaign travels ever took him close to her hometown he would like to meet her. As it happened, the young girl's father was one of the civic leaders in their small town, so when his daughter received a letter from Abraham Lincoln promising to visit her he shared the good news with other leaders in the town.

According to the story, Abraham Lincoln informed his staff that if his campaign train was scheduled to travel through that town he wanted to stop. It turned out that his schedule did include travel through that area, so the little girl (and all of the officials in the town, through her father) heard that Abraham Lincoln was coming to town!

When the day came, the vast majority of the small town gathered at the train station. Everyone was dressed up, the band was waiting—everyone except, it seemed, the little girl to whom Lincoln had written.

Just before the train arrived at the station, it had to stop for repairs. According to the version of the story I've heard, because the train was so close to the station, Lincoln decided to walk into town, and he took the little girl's address with him. He walked past the train station unnoticed, and through the somewhat deserted streets of the town until he found the little girl's house. He knocked on the door, introduced himself to the maid (who was speechless) and asked to see the little girl.

The little girl and a friend were having a pretend tea party. They invited the dignified Mr. Lincoln to join them. So he lowered himself to their level, sitting down on the floor, and they poured him make-believe tea into a little tea cup. After a while he asked the little girl if she liked his new beard, and then excused himself to walk back to his train.

When God in Christ harmonized the music of our lives to his own, he condescended to our level, so that we might know him. Remember that time when Jesus' disciples were trying to keep little children away from Jesus because they felt Jesus was just too busy to be bothered? Jesus told the disciples that unless they were changed and transformed so that they became like little children they would never enter the kingdom of heaven (Matthew 18:1-4). On another occasion Jesus said, "Let the little children come to me, and do not hinder them, for the kingdom of heaven belongs to such as these" (Matthew 19:14).

We can so easily fall for the idea that God is so busy with emergencies and high-level, far-reaching meetings and appointments he would never have time for us. But God is available, always and forever. He seeks us out, he finds our address and knocks on our door. He has time to drink pretend tea with us.

John 1:14: *The Word became flesh and blood, and moved into the neighborhood"* (The Message).

The Word got off the train and walked to our neighborhood. He has come to our house, demonstrating his love— he has truly gone the extra mile to harmonize our sour notes into his kingdom of heaven. God in Jesus reconciled himself to all things, and by not holding our sins against us God made peace with us on a cross that bleeds eternal forgiveness. If a voice in your head is telling you that God is not at peace with you, you can bet your bottom dollar that voice is not the voice of God.

The "done deal" nature of reconciliation poses a problem for institutionalized religion, of course, for it tends to put religion out of business. Religion and its programs and ceremonies sees itself as the middle man, the go-between, the intermediary between God and humans (sounds like one of the New Testament descriptions of Jesus' role in our lives, does it not?). Religion sees itself somewhat like the store, where the farmer (God) markets his produce for the consumer (that would be you and me). But the problem with that idea is that God *gives* his grace—it's Christ-less religion that is *selling* "salvation."

Market Economy Versus Gift Economy

Our North American culture is based on a market or barter economy. A market economy is based on *quid pro quo*—something given for a fair and equitable return for the effort or investment. Beyond our own culture and its economy, quid pro quo is the primary way that humans relate to each other. Early in life we learn that we must work for what we get. We discover that we earn wages for services we render. We earn approval and acceptance by deeds we perform. People like and love us if we help them, serve them and make them feel or look good.

A market economy, based on quid pro quo, is all about what we humans produce and accomplish. It's the way we make our own way and it's the way we build relationships with others. Religion is also based on quid pro quo. Religion preaches and practices quid pro quo as the way we can please and appease God. If we do something good for God, says performance-based religion, he will do something good for us.

On the other hand, God's grace proposes that spiritual goods and services are given without any agreement, contract or guarantee of immediate or future rewards. While few and far between, gift economies have existed in the history of this world. A successful life within such economies is not measured by the accumulation of material goods—within a physical, gift economy, the benchmark of a life well lived is seen as the degree to which one is able to pass on gifts to others. In the spiritual realm, embracing God's grace involves our willingness to yield ourselves as his servants so that his grace may be experienced by others.

Within physical gift economies, people come to trust that individual needs will be met by the cycle of giving—as everyone "pays forward" their blessings. For those of us who live in the dog-eat-dog, get-what-you-need-before-others-do high tech North American culture, a gift economy sounds hopelessly naïve. Such an idealistic way of life seems like it wouldn't work in our world.

You can see pockets of gift economies in individual families and smaller social units where gifts of time, money and resources are provided, without expectation of a return. Small mom and pop stores often have a container on the counter by the cash register with pennies and sometimes a nickel or dime or two. The idea is that you put in spare change from your transaction to help a later customer, whom you don't know, to pay the exact bill they owe, without having to "break" another bill.

Recently I stopped at a supermarket to quickly pick up two or three items we needed at home. As I hurried down the aisle to find what I wished to purchase, I thought how the average citizen of planet earth would react if they were to visit such a Disneyland-like market place of foods and beverages. I continued to mull that thought over as I arrived at the checkout counter, where the cashier informed me I owed $15.08.

I gave the cashier a $20 bill. He asked if I had eight cents. I fished for loose change in my pockets but found nothing. "Sorry," I replied. He smiled and said "no problem" and handed me a $5 bill in change. I was shocked. Someone was giving me more than I deserved! And this wasn't a small little mom-and-pop store—this was a chain, with rules, procedures and policies. I thanked him and left the store, wondering how that eight cents would be accounted for.

I couldn't get this unanticipated transaction, in my favor, out of my head. It was only eight pennies, but what if the cashier gave this same grace to other people? Would he lose his job? Walking through the parking lot, I determined that I must pass on the grace. When I arrived at my car, I retrieved some loose change from the ash tray and walked back into the store. Now it was the cashier's turn to be surprised. I gave him far more than the eight cents he gave me so that others might benefit from his generosity.

His small gift was an example of a gift economy in action. He helped me, and I in turn was motivated to help him to help others. It was a small transaction, but it was a kingdom of heaven transaction. I think that's the way a gift economy—both physically and spiritually—works.

A good friend of mine, the late Millard Fuller, founded Habitat for Humanity as well as the Fuller Center for Housing, based on a modified gift economy. Unpaid volunteers give of their time and talents, joining together to construct affordable housing for those who would otherwise be unable to own a home. The early New Testament church practiced a form of a gift economy—they "had everything in common" (Acts 2:44)—pooling their resources for the common good.

A physical or spiritual market economy encourages the hoarding and saving of goods and resources so that wealth can be increased. Wealth, in a market economy, is measured by physical possessions. In a gift economy, wealth actually decreases when one hoards their resources. Gift economies run on the principle that the circulation of a gift leads to personal increase—increase in relationships and increase in the moral fiber of the community at large.

I believe Jesus had such a pay-it-forward concept in mind when he gave his Parable of the Talents.

The Gift Economy in the Parable of the Talents

Matthew 25:21, 23: "His master replied, 'Well done, good and faithful servant!'"

These verses appear within the context of the parable of the talents. When these words are preached or read, people's minds often race into the future, imagining a time when they wait for their appointment to appear before God's throne of judgment. Inspired by what they think this passage means, they hope the moment they stand before God will find them having worked tirelessly, and finally, at the end, earning their heavenly Father's commendation.

This passage is often preached during "stewardship" drives, when church members are reminded of their responsibility to donate (or is it more like being guilted into giving?). The passage is thus abused, turning divine grace into human religious performance! The idea that we must work and work and work and then wait, on pins and needles, for the final judgment of God, hoping that he will say "well done" violates and corrupts the gospel of Jesus Christ!

Consider what the master actually means when he says, "Well done, good and faithful servant!"

We find the parable of the talents in Matthew 25:14-30. Jesus portrays a wealthy master as calling three servants together before he took a long trip. Jesus says that the master decided to give eight talents to his servants while he was gone.

The master then left, and while he was gone two of the servants *gained* more talents—doubling the amount they were given. The third servant "dug a hole in the ground and hid his master's money" (verse 18). The master then returned from this journey and *settled accounts* (verse 19) with the servants.

The bulk of the parable follows, consisting of a detailed conversation between the master and his three servants.

Matthew 25:20: Servant # 1—*"You entrusted me with five talents. See, I have gained five more."*
Matthew 25:22: Servant # 2—*"You entrusted me with two talents; see, I have gained two more."*
Matthew 25:24-25 Servant # 3—*"I knew that you are a hard man, harvesting where you have not sown.... So I was afraid and went out and hid your talent in the ground. See, here is what belongs to you."*

The master responds to the first two servants in the same way:

Matthew 25:21, 23: "Well done, good and faithful servant! You have been faithful with a few things; I will put you in charge of many things.... Come and share your master's happiness!"

The third servant completely misunderstood his master. He didn't perceive his master as loving and generous, but unforgiving and vindictive. The third servant was like many within Christendom today who perceive God as a harsh and stern taskmaster. The third servant accused his master of "harvesting where you have not sown" when, in fact, the master had given him the talent in the first place! They fear God like the third servant feared his master. The master has no words of praise for the third servant, but, within the context of what the servant didn't do with the talent he was given, calls the servant *wicked* and *lazy* (verse 26) and *worthless* (verse 30).

Here are some keys to keep in mind as we gain perspective on the gift economy of God—his amazing grace:

<u>Key #1</u>: **The master gave the talents**—the servants did not earn or deserve them. The talents were a gift, a sacred deposit of God's very own grace, which cannot be earned by human effort.

<u>Key #2</u>: **The master did not give equally**. The master did not give each of the three servants the same "mea-

sure" of his grace. They all received his grace—they all received his generosity— but in different "amounts" or degrees. The parable doesn't say that he was making this award based on their prior performance—it was simply a decision he decided to make.

Key #3: **The master expected the gifts he gave to be used**. The gifts he gave were to be shared, circulated, broadcast and distributed. He intended that these talents be "spread around." This parable comes back to the master's generosity and his determination to share what was his to begin with. The master gave them grace and he wanted to see his grace used and shared.

Key #4: **The servants weren't expected to produce more gifts**—likewise we are not expected to generate more grace, which is of course humanly impossible. No human can manufacture such a priceless and precious spiritual gift. The servants were (and are) simply asked to share his grace, because God's grace is dynamic—it grows as it is shared and passed on. The master merely asked that his servants become channels, conduits and vehicles of his grace. The master didn't want his grace returned (as the third servant thought)—he wanted it to be shared!

Key #5: – **When the master says "well done" he is not commending what his servants have produced by their own efforts**. Let's consider the master's praise, "well done." The central message of the parable of the talents is faithfulness. But whose faithfulness is commended? How are the first two servants able to exhibit that faithfulness?

What is the master conveying and communicating in saying "well done?" He is saying, "Well done, you have trusted me. Well done—you have accepted me. Well done—you have been faithful, because you have accepted my faithfulness, which in turn has empowered you to be a vehicle of my faithfulness. You are faithful because my faith lives in you. You love me because I first loved you. Well done!"

The message of grace is that we are all held in God's eternal embrace of love because of and through the faithfulness of Jesus Christ. We are *already* forgiven. We are *already* saved. We are *already* invited to his eternal banquet. We are *already* infinitely and eternally loved. God *already* loves us. Because of Jesus, God *already* says "well done" to us. Nothing we can do can separate us from the love of God, says Paul in Romans 8:39.

When the master, our heavenly Father says, "well done," he is choosing to see the obedience of Jesus, which he has imputed to us by his grace, in our lives. If our faithfulness depended on our humanly generated obedience, God would never say "well done" to any human, for we are not capable of achieving such a result, apart from him.

The parable of the talents is often abused by performance-based religion, offering it as an example of how humans might be saved by grace, but rewarded by works. When that interpretation is preached, the emphasis is often on "well *done*" as if that phrase directly connects our efforts with God's love and acceptance.

But such an interpretation completely misses the point of both the parable and the gospel! The parable does not specifically say that either one of the two servants whose gifts doubled did so as a result of their own diligent efforts. They simply told the master that they had gained the same number of talents as he had given them. How had they gained those talents? Well, we get a clue from the person who buried their talent in the ground. God's gifts are not meant to be buried. *We are not the end user of God's gifts.*

God's grace, specifically, cannot be bottled up and stored away in a "safe" place so that we and we alone may enjoy and profit from it. God's grace is dynamic—it defies anyone or any group who will try to hoard it for themselves. By virtue of accepting God's grace we realize that God will use us as an instrument to freely distribute his grace. In that way, the grace God gives us is multiplied. In God's gift economy, his grace is paid forward, distributed and multiplied. We grow in God's grace as we yield our lives as vehicles of his grace.

We will thus hear the praise "well done" from our master when we embrace his love, when we unconditionally accept his grace—when we give up our religious efforts of trying to prove to him how great we are, and instead cast ourselves on his faithfulness. His faithfulness will produce more grace through us. He rewards us when we allow him to use us to distribute and broadcast his grace—and such rewards are simply another gift, a reward God gives as the icing on the cake, the crown he places on top of his own gift of grace.

Our Dynamic Relationship With God

Paul, writing to Timothy, warned about "having a form of godliness but denying its power" (2 Timothy 3:5). The biblical Greek word for power is *dunamis*. Yes, that is the root of our English word dynamic! The "form of godliness" is the very same thing that troubled Jesus about religious leaders who washed only the outside of the cup, and who resembled whitewashed tombs filled with corruption. They are not what they appear to be. They are acting. That is what form without dynamic becomes. Empty hypocrisy. Religion for show.

God's grace is dynamic—it flows. It's more like a river than it is a lake or a reservoir. God's grace is not given to be held in trust in a religious safe deposit box. God's grace is not given so that we may bury it in a napkin and present it to the Lord upon his return, proving to him that we stored it up, saved it and never lost it. *God's grace is given to be given.* God's grace is a free flowing river—religion endeavors to be a reservoir of good deeds. God's grace grows as it is used, it is a gift which must be given, not merely to be replenished, but to grow. God's grace flows, whereas Christless religion, like the third servant in the Parable of the Talents, is intent on storage.

God's grace is the divine power that transforms us, from the inside out. However, accepting God's grace, and trusting in him, does not come easily. The Bible speaks of the purification process that produces a clean heart and a right spirit as being like a refiner's fire. God's grace is not the easy way out. God's grace, his *dunamis*, goes against the grain of our performance-based human spirit. The living water of God's grace transforms us, empowering us to "swim upstream" against the religious market economy of our world. Apart from God we resist his grace with every fiber of our being. We don't want to accept the humiliation of being dependent on God.

God's grace, the living water, flows to low places. God "opposes the proud, but gives grace to the humble" (1 Peter 5:5). God's grace flows to the humble, and it produces humility. God's grace is honest, real and authentic—it doesn't wear a religious mask. On the other hand, religious hypocrisy is a catastrophic attempt to bypass the process of facing our innate spiritual bankruptcy. The appearance of godliness is looking the look and talking the talk without surrendering to the risen Lord, who will produce true godliness in our lives.

The hollow tune of the teachers of the law and Pharisees haunts us still, and yet, if I am reading Jesus correctly, he is whistling along, improvising on our listless tedious theme, improvising a grace note now and again to see if we are listening. He is inviting us to allow him to live his life within us—giving power to lifeless shape, bringing dynamic to spiritually dead form. Jesus reconciles us, bringing us into harmony with God.

When we accept the love that God offers us, and are thereby reconciled to him, he steps into our lives and starts improvising so that we will begin to sing and play a new song—his song. His love renews us day by day (2 Corinthians 4:16)—transforming us from the kingdom of religion, transposing us, bringing us into harmony with the kingdom of heaven.

The new song of our lives is characterized by and defined by God's love. Love "comes from God. Everyone who loves has been born of God, and knows God" (1 John 4:7). God's love improvises us from what we were to what he wants us to be, his "new creation; the old has gone, the new has come!" (2 Corinthians 5:17). God translates us from the kingdom of religion into the kingdom of heaven. We are saved from all the misery and heartaches of our lives, so that in Christ we can become all that God wants us to be!

The new commandment of Jesus, the foundation and core teaching of his new covenant, is love (John 13:34-35). Paul tells us that "the fruit [singular] of the Spirit is love" (Galatians 5:22, my edit). There is only one fruit of the Spirit! Paul continues, telling us that love, the *fruit* of the Spirit, *is* "joy, peace, patience, kindness, goodness, faithfulness, gentleness and self-control" (Galatians 5:22-23). These attributes are not separate fruits, they are attributes of love—they flow out of the love that is produced by the Holy Spirit. These attributes are not objectives toward which we work and strive, hoping to develop more of them by prayer, fasting, Bible study, diligence and perseverance. Love is the gift of God!

*Ephesians 2:8-10: "For it is by grace **you have been saved**, through faith—and this not from yourselves, it is the gift of God— **not by works**, so that no one can boast. For we are God's workmanship, **created in Christ Jesus to do good works**, which God prepared in advance for us to do"* (emphasis mine).

• We are saved from the illusion that we are somehow capable of producing pleasing music for God. We are saved from the kingdoms of religion that insist we must march to their drum beat in order to be "saved."
• We are saved *by God's grace*—not by any of our own efforts.
• We are saved *by* grace *for* works—not the other way around! God steps into our lives so that he can improvise our lives, and create his new song in and through us—we are "created in Christ Jesus to do good works."

Here is one of the new songs, about Jesus, the Lamb of God, that is perpetually sung in the kingdom of heaven:

Revelation 5:9-10: "You are worthy to take the scroll and to open its seals, because you were slain, and with your blood you purchased men for God from every tribe and language and people and nation. You have made them to be a kingdom of priests to serve our God, and they will reign on the earth."

Jesus brought the kingdom of heaven to this earth. The power of the kingdom is his love—the covenant of the kingdom is love. God has already reconciled us—we have been saved—the kingdom of heaven is here now. The kingdom is Jesus—it's all about the love of God that he brought to this earth. Jesus taught his disciples, and all of us by extension, to pray "*your kingdom* come, your will be done on earth as it is in heaven" (Matthew 6:10, my emphasis).

Jesus brought heaven to earth. We often speak of going to heaven when we die. In some respects we do—heaven is where God is, and in death we are "at home with the Lord" (2 Corinthians 5:8). However, "going to heaven when we die" can become a cliché that reveals the failure of much of Christendom to embrace grace here and now.

There is no doubt that hell exists, here on planet earth, right now. Hell-on-earth experiences are being endured as I write these words and as you read them. But the flip side, the good news, is that the kingdom of heaven is alive and well on planet earth as well! Jesus came "to preach good news to the poor...to proclaim freedom for the prisoners and recovery of sight for the blind, to release the oppressed, to proclaim the year of the Lord's favor" (Luke 4:18-19).

The year of the Lord's favor is now—as soon as we accept it and embrace it. The doors of our prisons cells are now thrown open—we are invited to walk out of them, to live a new life in Christ. If we wish to be healed, we will be given spiritual vision that we may see Jesus, and embrace grace. Jesus beckons to us, offering us life in the Spirit, a new dimension. *God will go where religion dares not go.* God offers his love to all, without prejudice or prerequisites. God loves you, whether you like it or not—whether you choose to accept it or not! Embrace his grace!

I know of a Muslim chaplain who decided that he wanted to read the Bible. He studied it for months. In a group session with Christian chaplains he exclaimed, "Do you realize what a beautiful faith you have? What have you done to it?" Flabbergasted, the chaplains wanted to know what he meant.

He explained that what he read in our Bible seemed so disconnected from the message of Christian television and modern evangelicalism. He saw the beauty of grace, forgiveness, reconciliation and love in the Scriptures, but heard a different message in the Christian world.

To embrace grace is to reject Christ-less religion, and rejecting religion starts with embracing God's amazing grace.

Our Prayer:
Lord, forgive us of those times when we mess up the moment. By your grace, we are coming to know our own graceless patterns, with ourselves and with others. Help us to hear you transposing and transforming our messy tunes, right there in our worst moments, showing us that we are not alone, that you willingly enter our messes with a longing purpose—to show us how you will harmonize our lives so that we live in you, in real loving relationship. Transform our condemning choruses into your grace. And Lord, sing a new song in our lives, a song of forgiveness for those who have disappointed or hurt us, including religious institutions.